Using Earned Value

Using Earned Value

A Project Manager's Guide

ALAN WEBB

GOWER

Published by
Gower Publishing Limited
Gower House
Croft Road
Aldershot
Hants GU11 3HR
England

Gower Publishing Company
Suite 420
101 Cherry Street
Burlington, VT 05401–4405
USA

Reprinted 2006

Alan Webb has asserted his rights under the Copyright, Designs and Patents Act 1988 to be identified as the author of this work.

British Library Cataloguing in Publication Data
Webb, Alan
    Using Earned Value: A Project Manager's Guide
    1. Project management. I. Title
    658.4'04

ISBN 0 566 08533 X

US Library of Cataloguing in Publication Data
Webb, Alan
    Using Earned Value : A Project Manager's Guide / Alan
    Webb.
        p.   cm.
    1. Cost control. 2. Program budgeting. 3. Project management.
    I. Title.
    HD 47.33.W43 2003
    658.15'52–dc21   2002035441

Typeset in 9 point Stone Serif by IML Typographers, Birkenhead, Merseyside and printed in Great Britain by MPG Ltd, Bodmin, Cornwall.

Contents

List of Figures

List of Tables

Foreword

Earned value is coming of age. From its distant roots in work measurement at the dawn of the industrial revolution, earned value management has gone through many evolutions. Once the sole domain of the United States Department of Defense, earned value has now been adapted for use by commercial enterprises and governments around the world. This development parallels the path of project management, also undergoing its own evolution on the international stage. Once earned value was seen properly in the light of integrated project management and as the responsibility of the project manager, great strides were made in recognizing its core principles, thus making it even more adaptable to a broader range of projects.

Much of the criticism that has been levied on earned value in the past was due to an inflexible and dogmatic approach that was applied in the early days; however, recent developments in international standards and tireless work by its advocates have shown the world that the key principles are simply good project management techniques. The basic principles of managing projects with earned value are relatively easy to understand, if approached with common sense and the knowledge that earned value can and should be adapted to different environments and business cultures.

Earned value can sometimes be thought of incorrectly as the myriad of variance calculations and specialized terminology, but the mathematics is only one part of the equation. As Alan describes so well in this book, earned value enhances good project management through the development of integrated baseline planning and project control techniques. His discussion of alternative work breakdown structures will be of particular value to those commercial entities not bound by stricter government standards.

Alan also notes that perhaps one of the harder parts of using earned value is gaining acceptance from everyone from within the organization. But for those who have lived through the process, the insights gained from earned value management will forever change one's perspective on project management. Once a project manager has used earned value to manage a project, he will usually always want to manage with earned value.

While this book has been written primarily for project managers within the UK, it is my sincerest hope that this book will be a valuable resource and reference guide for project managers around the world, as earned value takes its rightful place within the project management community.

Eleanor Haupt
President, Project Management Institute's College of Performance Management
January 2003

Acknowledgement

Thanks are due to Eleanor Haupt, President of the Project Management Institute's College of Performance Measurement, for her invaluable advice and assistance with the preparation of this text. She took on the laborious job of reading the entire manuscript in detail and provided considerable insights into the evolution of earned value methods and current US practice that would have been almost impossible from this side of the Atlantic.

Alan Webb

Preface

I first became involved with earned value performance measurement back in the late 1970s, when I worked on a project to develop a major airborne weapons system that the United Kingdom was developing jointly with the United States. If it had not been for the US involvement, I have no doubt that earned value would never have been used and I would never have gained that initial experience. As things turned out, the US withdrew their support and a joint project became a purely national affair. With US funding taken out of the equation, things became very tight and it was time for a reappraisal; one of the first things that went was the earned value approach. No one mourned its demise, most were pleased to see it go, as it clearly cost a lot in terms of clerical effort for the information it produced.

The years passed and by the mid-1980s I was in the position of Senior Project Manager with a different company but still involved with airborne weapons development. Faced with new responsibilities in an increasingly harsh commercial climate, the whole question of the value being created by the project teams under my control grew in significance. It resulted in a number of personal initiatives including the introduction of a thorough value engineering programme and the use of earned value performance measurement. Despite the earlier experience, the ideas behind earned value management always seemed like the common-sense approach, but the problem was making it work without creating a complex and costly bureaucracy. At that time there were no books on the subject in the UK; what knowledge I had was from memory of the earlier application plus a sheet of formulae, and this turned out to be a big advantage. It freed me from all the conventional wisdom associated with the prescribed approach; instead it meant thinking the whole thing out in a way that would suit our method of working. Experience with the previous organization involving other computerized management systems also taught me that if systems were not designed to be integrated across all their interfaces at the start then getting them to work together sometime later would be a nightmare. As much as possible, interfaces had to be reduced to a minimum and data structures had to be both simple and universal. It also became clear that only a computerized approach would work with the limited staff available, so a search began for a suitable package. We were fortunate in that at the start of 1989 the first integrated project planning packages appeared that could perform earned value calculations. Implementation was generally trouble-free – the biggest point of contention was use of the new activity coding system which seemed alien to the older team members. Within two months of starting we were producing earned value reports on all new projects, although some projects at the mid-point of their lives were never converted to the new methods.

In many respects the systems that were introduced would not have conformed to the prescribed view of how earned value methods should be applied: there was no formalized Responsibility Assignment Matrix and the Work Breakdown Structure was of a completely new type but it worked and did everything I required. Senior management soon started taking note of the monthly reports and, taken together with the other initiatives, it raised awareness of cost and progress issues among all the project staff in a way that I believe no other approach would have done.

In the period since the early 1990s awareness of earned value methods has certainly grown and it has been greatly aided by the appearance of more project planning packages that contain earned value features. Nevertheless, very little has appeared in print about earned value in the United Kingdom; what has been written has generally appeared in the form of magazine articles which may be informative but do not say enough to provide a complete view. The only books that deal with the subject have been written in the USA with a specifically American market in mind. Unfortunately, they tend to endorse a procedure that is heavily influenced by a prescriptive, US government-inspired, approach to managing project contractors. As a result, anyone reading them might tend to believe that this is the only way that earned value can be used. In fact, nothing can be further from the truth; the earned value method can be used on projects of most types whether they are handled through contractors or are a purely internal affair. The method can be implemented as little more than an extension of the accounting process, or it can form part of a highly structured and formalized management control system, or it can be used in ways that lie between these two extremes. The important point is to recognize the project situation for what it is and use the earned value approach, not as a prescriptive process that has to be followed to the letter, but as an adaptable method and a valuable source of project data that provides as much information as you need, but no more.

In writing this book I hope that the reader will gain a greater insight into the whole process of earned value management whilst remaining free of the specifically American methodology that some will see as containing aspects that are unnecessary and inappropriate to their situation. However, I make no apology for the many references to American project history, practical experience, procedures and terms that appear in the pages that follow. It must be remembered that earned value management is an entirely US-inspired technique; all the original writings and specifications came from the US as do the commonly used terms and definitions. No proper discussion is possible without reference to these original works and the way they were implemented. They have shaped much of what followed and their influence still remains with us to this day.

Earned value principles of performance measurement are beginning to gain in popularity in the UK but it must be said that many organizations would be resistant to adopting the full US disciplines. That may be no bad thing as the United Kingdom is a nation that is known for taking the best of what it sees in foreign culture and practice, adapting it to suit itself and finally adopting it as its own. And so it may be with earned value techniques: this book may be the first that will be an original British contribution to this important subject and perhaps more will follow from around the world as the technique becomes widespread and new ways of using it are devised.

Alan Webb
Horsham, West Sussex, December 2002

1 Earned Value – What and Why

There cannot be many who practise in the field of project management who haven't brushed against earned value performance measurement at some point in their careers. For some it will be one of those techniques that was studied as part of a project management course but that was as far as it went, while for others it will be part of their normal project activities. One suspects that the latter group are still in the minority despite the fact that earned value methods have been around for about forty years. The obvious question must be why is it that a technique that has some real advantages for project managers has been largely ignored for so long, even though many in the profession are fully aware of it? Of course the answers are never simple but it cannot be denied that the technique gained a tarnished reputation from its early history and the way that it was first implemented in the United States. The popular view was that it was complex, bureaucratic, costly, peppered with alien terms and acronyms and something that one just wouldn't employ unless forced to do so. Not surprisingly, very little use was made of it outside the USA during its first thirty years but, since 1990, a more enlightened approach has developed along with suitable software tools that have made the technique appealing to a much wider audience.

The earned value principle is not difficult to understand – it comes from a basic concept that goes back to industrial engineering and accounting procedures that were around well before the discipline of project management arrived on the scene. Prior to the introduction of earned value methods, project managers were used to measuring the performance of their projects by reference to Gantt charts and Critical Path Analyses for the scheduling aspect, and the difference between the planned expenditure and the actual costs to see how the money was going. From a time dating back to the 1950s, it was realized that this was not a very satisfactory way of managing projects as there was always the problem of reconciling these two different measures of project progress. Furthermore, some highly influential customer organizations were embarrassed by cost overruns that never seemed to be predicted until it was too late to do anything but swallow hard and pay up. The answer they came up with was perfectly simple: make both a detailed plan and a detailed valuation of all the work in the project before you start, then, as the project progresses, make a note at each reporting point of 1) how much value should have been achieved according the plan, 2) how much value has been created according to the work done and 3) how much money has actually been spent. These values are shown in Figure 1.1. Those three numbers form the basis of all earned value methods; with a few simple mathematical ratios one can quickly judge the state of progress in terms of both the cost and the schedule. Anyone introduced to this idea for the first time would probably use terms such as 'obvious' or 'elementary' to describe such a basic concept, so it seems all the more baffling that it should not have received a more enthusiastic response. Some of the reasons have already been hinted at but like many good ideas there can be a wide gulf between theory and practice. Although simple in concept, the practice was much more complex because it was most often applied to projects that were very complex in themselves.

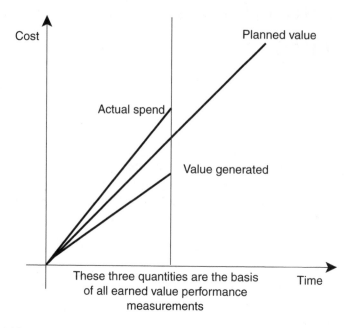

Figure 1.1   Adding the value generated as time passes gives a greater insight into the project than simply comparing the planned and actual values. The worth in financial terms associated with the value generated is termed the 'earned value'

Earned value methods had something of an unfortunate start that has never helped the process gain wide acceptance. In those early days, earned value was not seen as a performance measurement system in its own right to be used and adapted as required; instead it was introduced as part of a much larger and highly prescriptive government initiative. In the first incidence, this was the US Department of Defense's PERT/Cost system which proved to be a significant failure; that experience alone coloured the next thirty years' contracting practice. Next it was used more successfully on the Minuteman programme and finally it was incorporated in a US DoD project management specification that detailed the Cost/Schedule Control Systems Criteria. This important document made a provision for earned value measurement and reporting but it was wrapped up in a logical but bureaucratic management process that was designed to meet the particular needs of the DoD. The fact was that few people made the distinction between the earned value accounting and measurement principles and the total system in which it was contained. As the principal market for earned value methods was among the contractors to the DoD and the only documents that explained the procedure were the government specifications, the perception spread that this was the 'right', 'official' or 'only' way that earned value could be applied. It is perhaps not surprising that the rest of the world viewed it as a quirk of US business practice and took little notice.

It might just have remained that way if it had not been for the PC revolution of the 1990s when a new breed of project planning software burst onto the market. A break from the stand-alone systems of earlier generations, the new software allowed integration with other company systems and also contained earned value calculations. These systems were not based on government requirements but instead recognized that earned value performance measurement is actually a process that springs from the integration of a planning system with an accounting system. Freed from the US government-inspired approach to total project control, project managers using suitable project planning software packages could begin to use earned value performance measurement as a valuable project control tool but in ways that suited themselves. It was at this point that earned value finally 'came of age'.

What sort of projects suit earned value methods?

Any project with a structured plan of work, a cost structure and a suitable data-gathering system can make use of earned value methods but it would be unreasonable to suggest that the approach is equally applicable to all types of project. In general, projects that are well suited to earned value methods are those which have most or all of the following characteristics:

- a clearly defined objective
- a clearly perceived route to the goal
- work taking place over an extended period
- a high labour content
- tasks of a creative nature
- a formalized management structure
- cost and time limitations.

An ideal application is engineering development work and it was on projects of that type that the first use of earned value was made.

Without a clearly defined objective no one can say what route the project might take or where it might end up; it may at some point focus on an objective, in which case effort will be concentrated upon it or it may lose sight of any real objective and be terminated. Projects of this type cannot be controlled in any formal sense; what plans are made are likely to be short-term or subject to constant variation and no proper performance measurement is possible even though data may be gathered about expenditure and work.

All performance measurement relies on the idea of a clearly perceived plan that takes the project from inception to the attainment of the goal. Some projects cannot be planned in detail because the route contains many uncertainties that can only be resolved at the time they are confronted. This can occur with projects that contain a large research element where the outcome of any experiments cannot be known in advance and the outcome may determine what new lines of enquiry are pursued. It can also apply in an opportunistic situation where the project strategy might include taking advantage of what opportunities arise, for example, where sales to third parties, or the involvement of outside parties, is involved. Without a stable plan in which all can have confidence, earned value performance measurement is not suitable.

Performance measurement demands a planning, a monitoring and a data-gathering process. In practice, data gathering and processing take time; in large companies or large projects, the time-scales can run into weeks or even months before accurate data becomes available. Projects looking to use earned value methods for control and forecasting should take note of the actual reporting time-scales; if the projects are of short duration with respect to the reporting cycle, the performance measurement data may be of little use for actual control although it may have some historical and statistical value. With short-duration projects, more direct control techniques may be more suitable.

Earned value was conceived as a method of valuing work done. Although purchased items or materials are not excluded from the earned value approach, this aspect was not the principal focus. If a project is to consist primarily of purchases with very little labour (for example, a project that consists of the purchase of a suite of standard equipment amounting to 90 per cent of the project value, with the only labour element being the installation and commissioning) then earned value methods would have little real impact as a control mechanism. In a case such as this, control would be much better exercised through the pricing agreement with the supplier, which might include discounts, incentives or liquidated damages for late delivery.

The first applications of earned value methods were on major defence engineering development projects. As such, these projects contain a high degree of innovation involving problems which demand a creative solution. These kind of projects are among the most risky and are prone to schedule and cost overruns. Earned value methods were devised to deal with such problems, in particular, to generate some objective measures of progress in a somewhat unstable project situation. Whereas there is no absolute reason why earned value methods cannot be used on routine projects with little creative demand, the question becomes: is it really worth doing? In situations that are largely repeats of earlier well-understood projects, in which there is little risk at the start, or are mostly repetitive production-type operations, then earned value methods are not likely to be of great benefit. Control might be better exercised through simple progress recording and fixed price contracting arrangements which should be easy to agree if things are well known at the start.

Without a formalized management structure, there is not much point in attempting performance measurement unless one is only interested in statistics. Earned value management implies not only a well-defined plan against which performance can be measured, but that someone is going to take responsibility for implementing the plan, take note of the performance measurement results and carry out whatever actions are indicated. If no proper management structure exists or the relationships are only vaguely defined, it may prove impossible to obtain objective information about progress, as well as getting anyone to be responsible for achievement. It may be possible to implement an earned value system of sorts if the planning and data-gathering aspects exist, but the results will have little practical value in terms of the influence they exert over progress.

Another name for earned value management is 'integrated cost and schedule control', because it brings together a way of measuring achievement against both time and cost goals. If a project has neither of these limitations within the control horizon or the cost limit cannot be tied to any particular work or outcome, then earned value methods are not appropriate. Examples of projects of this type are found in long-term research and development, for example, finding a cure for certain types of cancer: it could take five years or it might take ten – and nobody knows.

The case for implementing earned value methods is no different from the case for implementing any other management technique: it is quite simply an economic one. There is always a cost associated with obtaining any information on a project and the issue is one of deciding whether the costs are going to bring the required benefits. In fact, it is not possible to answer that question as the decision must be made before the project starts and no one can say what extra costs might be incurred on the project or what overruns might occur if earned value is not employed. So it becomes a question of what type of project is most suitable, and the answer is given above: if a project does not fit a substantial part of this profile then other methods might be more suitable, and some suggestions about what to use have been made.

How sophisticated do we have to be?

Earned value methods were first embodied in some highly detailed US government specifications that appeared in the 1960s. Since then, earned value has been applied across a range of industries and in different ways; Figure 1.2 shows a contemporary US view. Some of the terms shown in the diagram may be unfamiliar and more explanation is given in later chapters but the overall view is clear. Figure 1.2 makes an important point: far from being a prescriptive process that can only be done in one way, earned value management should be adapted to needs as determined by the scale of the project and the organization undertaking it. At the left-hand end, we have small organizations and comparatively simple projects, in this case the core earned value accounting principles and simple reports will be sufficient. At the extreme right-hand end, we have very large projects that are the province of the US government departments such as the Department of Defense and here compliance will be required with a national standard for earned value management, incorporating 32 criteria that define the process. Whereas this situation is not directly applicable to the United Kingdom, as no UK government department demands compliance with a US national standard, the principle remains the same. Simpler projects can use a simplified approach, while more costly and complex projects need a more rigorous procedure.

	Commercial or Defence		US Government	Major contractors
Where	Small companies	Larger companies	organic	to the US DoD
When	As required	Corporate policy	DoD non-major contracts (>12 months) >$6.3m	DoD major contracts > $73, TDT&E >$315m Prod
Reports	Streamlined, simple	Tailored to needs	Simplified C/SSR	Detailed CPR
Method	Core EV principles	Tailored applications	Full compliance with ANSI/EIA-748-1999 All $values Fiscal Year 2000	

Figure 1.2   The range of application of earned value principles as seen in the USA. Note that only the largest defence contract would be viewed as requiring the rull rigours of ANSI/EIA-748-1998 criteria compliance (Source: Eleanor Haupt)

What can we expect from earned value?

When earned value was first introduced there is no doubt that the sponsors were looking for a much better insight into the progress of their projects from both a cost and a schedule standpoint than they had before. In particular they did not want any nasty surprises from contractors making sudden demands for more money and increased time without any clear warning that the project situation was deteriorating. That situation has not altered; it is as important today as it was forty years ago to have a clear view of how well a project is doing and where it is heading. Its importance appears in a number of ways:

- Early warning of a deteriorating situation creates an opportunity to do something about it before it is too late.
- Accurate forecasting allows better decisions to be made about the course of the project.
- Accurate forecasting allows better decisions to be made about matters outside the project which may be influenced by the progress of the project.
- An open and verifiable view of progress improves sponsor confidence.

These are all good reasons why earned value performance measurement is an important project management technique but there can be additional benefits. Earned value methods demand effective planning, costing and monitoring systems; the emphasis placed on these aspects can improve overall project management through the discipline they bring. Furthermore, management using earned value techniques requires a proper system of controls with the appropriate allocation of responsibility for achievement.

In 1994, a survey was carried out in the United Kingdom among users of earned value methods; one question was what benefits have users experienced through the implementation of this approach? The response is shown in Figure 1.3. The most striking feature is the broad range of benefits that are claimed and the high incidence among the respondents for some of the most important features. Not surprisingly, all claimed to have seen much better integration of costs and plans but over 80 per cent also saw improved cost forecasting and earlier sight of problems, both of which are important benefits in their own right. Two-thirds noted better financial control and, most importantly, better overall management awareness of the project situation. As to actually making a reduction in the overall project cost through the use of earned value, only one-third claimed to have seen any evidence of this but this is a difficult issue as it is not possible to say what costs might have arisen if earned value methods had not been used.

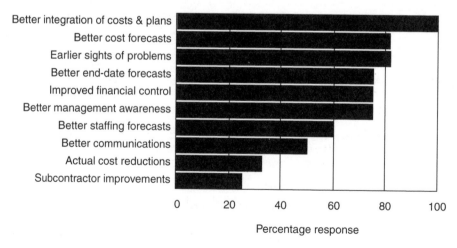

Figure 1.3   Benefits associated with earned value methods as seen in a British survey

Earned value methods come at a price; there is no doubt that introducing them in a project environment can be a significant complication compared to running a project without them. They can call for changes to operating practices that go well beyond producing a few new reports as they can demand much greater discipline within the planning process, much greater emphasis on objective reporting, improved integration between the planning systems and the accounting systems, and they might even require new software to be installed. Inevitably there can be problems when a new approach is introduced, particularly when it can demand changes such as those mentioned, but the benefits are well worth having. It is a significant fact that of the companies surveyed, none was contemplating abandoning the practice; once the initial problems had been overcome, the experience encouraged some of the organizations to make more widespread use of the technique.

2 Origins and History

The fundamental ideas that have come to form the earned value approach to project control stem from two distinct lines of thought: those that originated with industrial engineers and those that come from project managers. Industrial engineers wishing to measure the performance of production lines realized, perhaps as far back as the nineteenth century, that three measures were needed to establish how well and cost-effectively the manufacturing process was working. They created the concept of a 'cost standard'; that is, the amount of cost or value to be attributed to a single unit of output. This is a very important measure as it is usually based on a detailed study of the labour content, charge rates, overhead structure, material content and their associated costs. Such figures are vital when it comes to both product pricing and the expected profitability of the production process. To assess the efficiency of the production line in operation, they counted the number of items actually made, compared it with the planned or expected number of items to be made and finally, from the material accounts, the time bookings and the current overhead rates, they worked out the actual costs incurred. Applying the cost standard to the actual and planned output figures generated standard costs that could be compared with the actual costs. Three figures were generated:

- the planned output at standard cost rates
- the actual output at standard cost rates
- the actual cost incurred.

Comparing these figures led to the ideas of:

- process efficiency – actual output at standard cost compared to planned output at standard cost
- cost efficiency – actual output at standard cost compared to actual incurred cost.

If either of these measures showed a poor position then the profitability of the process was in doubt and something needed to be done. The actual output at standard cost is what has come to be known as the 'earned value', that is, what has actually been produced at the cost you expected to pay.

A government initiative

Until the advent of Critical Path Methods (CPMs) in the late 1950s, projects were viewed in a very different light from production processes; they were unique undertakings for which no standards could be established, and certainly not from long-term observation and measurement. Critical path methods (CPM) and PERT (Program Evaluation and Review technique) methods were the first systematic attempt to plan projects in detail and control progress through rational analysis and decision making. Planning charts of the Gantt type had been used for at least fifty years before that time but the analytical approach was lacking. CPM and PERT relied on high-speed computers which were just making their entrance into business operations; with hindsight perhaps too much faith was placed in just what these methods were really capable of doing with the technology then available. It was realized at the time the PERT system was invented that if cost rates could be added to the hours and durations that are attached to project activities, a powerful system would exist for predicting and, ultimately, controlling the costs of projects. The US Department of Defense (DoD) and the National Aeronautics and Space Administration (NASA), as the largest instigators of projects involving the highest technical risks, saw the immediate application of the idea; in 1962 they sought to impose the system on their major contractors under the title PERT/Cost. This approach contained the 'earned value' concept as now it was possible to draw an analogy with the industrial engineer's approach. One could see the plan in terms of its anticipated costs and the accounting system should provide the actual expenditure, all that was needed was a way of valuing the work done and, in theory, this should be a relatively simple process: 'A comparison of the actual costs accumulated to date and the contract estimate for the work performed to date will show whether the work is being performed at a cost which is greater or less than planned.'[1]

However, the DoD's application was very heavy-handed, as it specified the total costing system that was to be used throughout the project. The result was a complete rejection by an industry that had already made large investments in its accounting systems and was not about to change to a new and untried method, especially as the required software had barely been developed. By 1965 PERT/Cost was dead and so too was PERT as industry found them too demanding and by and large preferred the simpler CPM which did not require the three-estimate method inherent in PERT.

All this happened at a time when some very high-profile US aircraft development projects, notably the C-5A Galaxy freighter and the F-111 bomber, were experiencing major cost and schedule overruns that seemed to come out of the blue. There was a suspicion that the true picture had been deliberately obscured until it was too late to do anything about it, which was a major embarrassment to the DoD civil servants in charge of procuring these systems. The DoD was clearly open to criticism if it had to keep going back to Congress to ask for more money on projects that should have been reasonably straightforward if properly conceived at the start. Concurrent with these two programmes was the Minuteman anti-missile system development project and for this a special reporting system had been set up. This was called the Minuteman Contractor Performance Measurement system; Devised by Brigadier General Samuel Phillips, it embodied the earned value principle of performance assessment against a fixed 'baseline' plan but without any of the complex systems and planning requirements of PERT/Cost, and it appeared to be more successful. In particular, it did not require the detailed activity costings that were a feature of the network-based PERT approach but relied on higher-level work packages that were derived from another important data set: the Work Breakdown Structure. Realizing a serious mistake had been made in the handling of the introduction of the new management processes, the DoD and NASA decided that a less rigid approach would be more appropriate; in particular it would allow industry to choose its own management methods and software tools providing it met a series of criteria that were deemed to be good management practice. These were finally embodied in a US Department of Defense Instruction DODI 7000.2 of 22 December 1967 called 'Performance

Measurement for Selected Acquisitions'. The title gives the clue to what this instruction was really intended to do, in particular it was about *performance measurement* (that is, visibility of progress in plain terms), *selected*, implying that this was not to be a blanket procedure applied to all DoD programmes, and *acquisitions* as this was to be used on acquisition programmes (that is, projects that were to create new products to be acquired by the DoD). Projects such as long-term R&D were excluded. The title does not suggest that project performance would actually be improved by the use of this instruction although that clearly must have been a hope. One suspects that what was uppermost in the minds of the DoD managers was:

- visibility of what they were getting for what they were paying
- measurement rather than guesswork
- no more embarrassment due to contractors concealing the real position of the project.

DODI 7000.2 set out what were to be known as the Cost/Schedule Control Systems Criteria (C/SCSC),[2] popularly called the 'C-Spec'. In many ways it was a seminal work in the evolution of project management as it set a precedent for much of what has followed, so much so that its methodology has acquired a stature that is above its real place among some practitioners who have perhaps forgotten or never knew its original purpose. Earned value reporting was a part of this standard but it included another important feature: data structuring. The structure it set out is not, however, essential for earned value measurement but it has become inextricably linked to it in the eyes of some advocates, and possibly the project management profession as a whole, which has in turn obscured the real position.

DODI 7000.2 was not a lengthy document, the core of it consisted of 35 simply stated criteria such as:

The contractor's management control systems will include policies, procedures and methods which are designed to ensure that they will accomplish the following:

a) Organization
1) Define all authorized work and related resources to meet the requirements of the contract using the framework of the CWBS (Contract Work Breakdown Structure)
2) Etc.

b) Planning and Budgeting
1) Schedule all authorized work in a manner which describes the sequence of work and identifies the significant task interdependencies required to meet the development, production and delivery requirements of the contract
2) Identify physical products, milestones, technical performance goals or other indicators that will be used to measure output
3) Etc.

c) Accounting
1) Record direct costs on an applied or other acceptable basis in a formal system that is controlled by the general books of account.
2) Summarize direct costs from the cost accounts into the WBS without allocation of a single cost account to two or more WBS elements.
3) Etc.

d) Analysis
1) Identify at the cost account level on a monthly basis using data from, or reconcilable with, the accounting system:
   a) Budgeted cost for work scheduled and budgeted cost for work performed
   b) Budgeted cost for work performed and applied (actual where appropriate) direct cost for the same work
   c) Etc.[3]

The above extracts give an idea of the standard; although much of it can be considered as a sensible approach to managing a project, it was both prescriptive and demanded a great deal of bureaucracy. In addition to the basic criteria there was a requirement for highly detailed reporting in precisely defined formats (DODI 7000.10: C/SCSC Reports). As if that was not enough, the US DoD developed hundreds of detailed questions about how a company functioned and sent audit teams to ensure contractor compliance. The teams sometimes adopted an over-zealous attitude that did not lend itself to the general acceptance of the methods on the part of industry, particularly as many of the questions were considered to be commercially sensitive, marginal to the central issue of managerial control and really none of the DoD's business. The scene was thus set for an uneasy relationship between the government and its contractors. In practice, the implementation of DODI 7000.2 was slow and by 1972 only 36 contractors had been certified as compliant; it was generally regarded by industry as both DoD interference and costly bureaucracy.

System problems

During the 1960s, the majority of project cost on DoD-type projects was attributable to labour and, using time-booking systems that were common in all companies, planned, earned and actual labour cost could be relatively simply calculated providing the time records could be related directly to the plan. The same was not true of the material aspects of the project. Whereas practically all companies with a procurement system can produce two basic figures – the budgeted cost for material purchases and the actual cost of materials purchased – few can produce an 'earned' value of materials at any point in the process. This is because the value of materials can vary with time due to a host of factors such as the effects of inflation, the effects of different batch sizes, price changes in the market, etc., but the DODI instruction demanded that all these variations be accounted for on a continuous basis through a series of tracking points. Things got even more difficult when materials were bought in large quantities which could be used on a variety of development projects as well as on routine production work. Needless to say, material accounting under earned value methods was a painful process: 'firms had to create new or substantially modified material accounting systems to comply with the criteria'. That might have been all to the good but experience has proved 'there is very little relationship between what is required to provide for an efficient contractor procurement system and the satisfaction of those criteria which impact materials'.[4] In other words, operating an earned value type of material accounting system does little or nothing for creating an efficient purchasing arrangement, it can simply lead to heavy and expensive systems. However, one must remember that the DoD had been stung by embarrassing, unforeseen overruns; in the Cold War climate of the 1960s, with its heavy emphasis on defence, it was willing to pay the high costs of the bureaucracy.

Despite the difficulties, contracting companies began using the approach and this led to two important developments. First, software companies started to produce package systems that would support the C/SCSC requirements, do the earned value calculations and generate the highly detailed reports. Second, a body of knowledge began to accumulate about the performance of projects that were run under earned value conditions. Unsurprisingly, commercial industry that may have become aware of the C/SCSC approach had no inclination at all to follow the lead; some progressive firms adopted earned value accounting principles for reasons of their own but without the inherent bureaucracy contained in the criteria. In 1975 the US Department of Energy adopted a broadly similar approach with a C/SCSC contracting arrangement for its major projects but beyond that no other government departments in the USA or elsewhere took much interest in earned value until the 1990s. It is significant that the UK Ministry of Defence has been well aware of the methods but has never imposed a C/SCSC contractual arrangement on its contractors, although it now advocates the use of earned value management principles where appropriate.

The consultant's view

Inevitably, a complex system like C/SCSC had its critics: senior people in both industry and government argued that if the DoD really wanted to save money on its projects it should abandon the C/SCSC process. The DoD took this criticism seriously; 15 years after the introduction of DODI 7000.2 it commissioned consultants Arthur D. Little to conduct an independent enquiry into its usefulness and whether it was worth the additional costs it was clearly having to pay. Arthur D. Little reported in 1984, having taken evidence from both the government side and industry. The report concluded that both sides agreed that using C/SCSC was effective as a project control mechanism and the benefits outweighed the costs. However, there were sharply differing views from industry and government about the details of how it was implemented. The main, and well-voiced, criticisms from industry were that 1) the prescribed approach required far too much detailed reporting and variance analysis, much of which was of too low a level to be of use for overall control, and 2) the requirement to maintain the baseline position, when work-around plans were what was really needed, was too restrictive for effective control. The government criticisms were much less cohesive and to some extent at odds with each other, indicating (surprisingly, as it was a government-inspired scheme) that they had lost sight of the original objectives while failing to appreciate what was practical and achievable. The study reported: 'In summary, effective internal management does not of itself require detailed reporting to the government. However, reporting to the government should be expected as a reality of doing business with the government, particularly when the work entails cost risk to the government. The government need for information is not always taken into account by contractors.'[5] This statement reveals the whole position and purpose of the C/SCSC approach; if you simply substitute the word 'sponsor' for 'government' you can apply this more generally. In short, the C/SCSC process is in place primarily for the benefit of a sponsor who is paying a contractor, or group of contractors, to undertake a project on his behalf, who is also bearing both the cost and schedule risks – and expects to be kept well informed. It also makes a tacit admission that if it were not for the requirements of the government, industry would run its projects more cheaply and simply. Other complaints covered the unnatural and complex approach required to handling material costs, the competence and narrow-mindedness of personnel on the audit teams and the unrealistically short time-scales that were allowed for the development of a realistic baseline plan. As both sides felt there were sufficient advantages to retain the general approach, Arthur D. Little's recommendations contained nothing fundamental and were largely confined to administrative matters covering organization, training and some points of operation.

A new direction for the 21st century

From a US government perspective, the C/SCSC method must be considered a success, even if the old delays and overruns persist. The imposition of the criteria improved contractor awareness of good project management practice in a way that might not have come about by pure competitive pressure. However, there has been a comparative failure, until recently, to get earned value methods into the commercial world. This situation has been greatly influenced by 1) its somewhat tarnished reputation as costly and bureaucratic, which stemmed from the early days and the DoD's approach, and 2) doubts about its applicability in a commercial environment that is increasingly looking to fixed price contracting and the imposition of liquidated damages as a way of containing cost and schedule overruns.

By the early 1990s the DoD, which had been so instrumental in formulating and promoting the earned value approach with its strict compliance criteria, began to realize that its acquisition processes had placed too much emphasis on adherence to fixed plans and reporting in detail against them rather than emphasizing doing things in the most efficient way. Although it was getting plenty of data about *earned value*, what was not so clear was that what it was buying represented *good value* for the money it was paying. Even more pointedly, many items purchased for military use were found on examination to be little different, if not identical, to items that were available to commercial industry at a fraction of the cost. In 1996, the DoD issued new directives in the DOD 5000 series that completely changed the emphasis from one of detailed control at every level to a total system acquisition process that made compliance with user needs, effective integration of complex systems and best value products, the principal programme drivers. Gone was the old adversarial approach between government and industry, to be replaced with the formation of 'Integrated Product Teams' and the beginning of a new partnership.

A revolution in the approach to earned value came in 1993 when Gary Christle from the Office of the Under Secretary of Defense set out a plan for reform in five key areas:

- Change the emphasis from the government to the contractor. Compliance with C/SCSC should be based upon how the contractor actually manages rather than an imposed view. Rather than automatic reviews and audits imposed by contract awards, C/SCSC reviews would only be required if there was poor discipline or faulty certification.
- Reduce the amount of surveillance required by both the government and contractor.
- Put earned value in its proper context as an integrating tool for cost, schedule, and technical management; this changed the emphasis from reporting on earned value to managing with earned value.
- Limit and tailor reporting to what can and will be effectively used.
- Ensure comprehensive planning and common understanding by both parties through the implementation of a baseline review after contract award.

Several other significant changes occurred. Ownership of the policy for earned value was transferred from the comptroller's office to the acquisition policy office, thus signalling that the project managers, not the accountants, owned the process and the policy. A policy directive was soon issued that changed the focus of earned value reviews from auditing the processes (the old C/SCSC compliance reviews) to integrated baseline reviews that were conducted jointly by the government and contractor. The DoD underscored its determination to ensure industry ownership of the process by asking five industrial associations to propose industry-standard guidance to replace the 35 original criteria.

In 1996, industry responded with a standard that reduced the original 35 criteria to 32 (see Appendix 2). Overall, it was broadly similar; with the exception of three criteria which were deleted, there is general equivalence on the remaining 32. However, certain important changes were incorporated which recognized that the needs of commercial industry were somewhat different to those of government. In particular, there were two very significant changes: 1) the Work Breakdown Structure was no longer required to be a product-based one expressed in terms of contract deliverables, but a structure that was compatible with the management methods in use, and 2) the material cost reporting system was to be one that accorded with normal industry practice. Overall, the emphasis across the criteria was changed from strict adherence to procedure to one of using the most suitable and managerially efficient methods in the circumstances. In December 1996, the 32 industry criteria formally replaced the old 35 with the DoD 5000.2R regulations and industry was left to find processes that were suitable to managing the job effectively. The 32 criteria were later incorporated in an Earned Value Management commercial standard ANSI/EIA-748-1998 which was approved in May 1998 and this was adopted in 1999 as the official DoD approach, completing the demise of the old ways. The official announcement stated:

> The guidelines in this document are purposely high level and goal oriented as they are intended to state the qualities and operational considerations of an integrated manage-ment system using earned value analysis methods without mandating detail system characteristics. Different companies must have the flexibility to establish and apply a management system that suits their management style and business environment. The system must, first and foremost, meet company needs and good business practices.[6]

This swept away the supporting checklist of questions which had become detailed criteria in their own right and left the original authors' intent standing in the 32 criteria. Gone were the days of C/SCSC compliances reviews and audits with excessive demands for compliance with the criteria. By stating that different companies need to define for themselves management systems that suit their management style and business environments, the DoD had recognized after thirty years a fundamental truth about project management as a process. Rigid procedures, however logical and well intended, are no guarantee of efficiency, in fact they can be quite the opposite. To be efficient, firms must know how to choose from the available range of systems and techniques those methods that will be effective in the particular circumstances of the project and apply them in a way that makes a real contribution to project success. This means a flexible or adaptive approach that always keeps the ultimate goal of the project firmly in mind and tailors everything to that end. Of course, many contractors who had developed systems that were both C/SCSC compliant and managerially useful continued to use them in the new environment; many have used earned value methods as a primary component of their business management methodology and find it effective.

The C/SCSC legacy

Earned value, as a method of calculation of project performance, is an accounting principle; it actually relies on comparatively little project information, but earned value was only one aspect of the criteria that were set out in DODI 7000.2 as it specified a total approach to project management. Important features of DODI 7000.2 such as the Work Breakdown Structure and the Cost Accounts are not essential to performing earned value calculations (if one is only interested in accounting data), but a good planning system and a compatible cost-reporting system are essential and they must be in place and working. This point was not actually overlooked but it was de-emphasized due to the DoD's failure when it tried to impose the use of the half-developed PERT/Cost system, an approach which made those requirements very clear. There was so much trepidation over this point that the planning system, which is really fundamental to effective earned value methods, was left out of the principal data structure; there was no requirement to use a PERT-like networking system and some contractors chose not use networks. Instead, it placed emphasis on 1) data structuring that was based on product and work visibility, 2) accountability for achievement, and 3) highly detailed reporting. Inevitably, this approach has found its way into the special software packages that have been developed. For the most part, these were created to serve the contractors to the DoD and DoE as these were the only markets and thus followed the very prescriptive format. The legacy of DODI 7000.2 is still with us in the form of the specialist earned value software tools and the 'conventional wisdom' of how earned value should be applied.

UK experience

In the United Kingdom, very little use was made of earned value methods during the 1970s and 1980s due to both ignorance of the method and lack of suitable software. Some firms did adopt the principles using systems they created themselves; unless a firm happened to be a contractor to the US DoD there was simply no reason to adopt the US approach. It has already been pointed out that the earned value principle is more dependent on a planning system and a cost-reporting system than it is on work breakdown structures (WBS) even though that feature first got earned value off the ground. Throughout the 1980s, there was an explosion in the development of project management planning packages due, in part, to the development of personal computers. These new packages were much more versatile than the old cumbersome systems and allowed the integration of planning data with other systems such as time bookings and accounts. Once this had been achieved, elementary earned value calculations became possible and by the early to mid-1990s many of the popular planning packages offered earned value information as part of the report suite, although the report formats were not compliant with the DoD requirements. Figure 2.1 gives an example of a report from 1990 showing basic earned value data in a project status report. In some packages, however, the use of the basic terms was not quite the same as in the original definitions and derived formulae; this has unfortunately led to some confusion and possible mistrust of the information derived. Some early systems, it must be said, also contained basic errors in the calculations.

By the mid-1990s, there were still very few companies in the UK using earned value methods but a small number were surveyed by a group of students working for this author.[7]

PRESTIGE PC	EARNED VALUE – VARIANCES & INDICES	PAGE NUMBER : 1
		RUN DATE : 12Apr90
PROJECT: PROJECT DEFINITION STUDY	REPORT AC03	TIME NOW : 31Mar90
		FORECAST END : 06Dec90
		REQUIRED END : 31Aug90

VERSION 00

DRAWING OFFICE: PHASE 1

ACTIVITY IDENT. / DESCRIPTION	ACTUAL TO DATE	EARNED VALUE	BUDGET SCHEDULED	SCHEDULE VARIANCE	COST VARIANCE	SCHEDULE PERF. INDEX	COST PERF. INDEX
12310 D. O. MANAGEMENT	.00	.00	1490.40	−1490.40	.00	.00	
12320 D. O. -SCHEME CONTROL PANEL	247.77	275.30	275.30	.00	27.53	1.00	1.11
12321 D. O. -SCHEME LOOM LAYOUT	1624.27	1569.21	1569.21	.00	−55.06	1.00	.97
12322 D. O. -SCHEME NEW CASING	853.43	853.43	853.43	.00	.00	1.00	1.00
12327 D. O. SCHEME FINAL DESIGN	00.0	00.0	00.0	.00	.00		
TOTALS	4157.03	4074.44	8070.07	−3995.63	−82.59	.50	.98

Figure 2.1 An example of an earned value progress report from *Prestige PC* dating from 1990. Note the cost and schedule performance indices

The survey found that the reasons for introducing earned value methods were rather various and some commented that they had found some difficulty in getting things to work. All indicated that they had achieved much better integration between costing and planning than before but few felt that they had achieved any overall cost reductions on their projects due to earned value being implemented. However, every respondent felt that once the system was working there were benefits and none was contemplating abandoning the approach.

Around the world, some government departments started to realize the worth of the earned value method and began mandating its use for their contracts. One notable example was the Australian defence department which is now demanding earned value reporting, causing some British suppliers of defence equipment to formally implement the process. The advent of the Internet has also had its effect and there is now a major website devoted to earned value methods which contains much useful information: <www.acq.osd.mil/pm/>. It also shows that a sizeable community of earned value practitioners has grown up, although the correspondence on the notice board tends to indicate that it is mostly contained within the USA. The correspondence also tends to indicate that there is 1) still some confusion surrounding the terms and calculations, 2) continuing doubt about the applicability of earned value to specific situations, particularly fixed price contracting, 3) difficulty with the minutiae of dealing with the reporting requirements in a full earned value management (EVM)-compliant environment and 4) difficulty with the use of certain software packages.

The problems outlined above are not surprising, given both the diverse nature of projects and the inevitable complexity associated with a system that ties together cost and schedule aspects of a project that might previously have been treated separately. However, progress is being made: the old prescriptive methods have been replaced with a more flexible approach that will surely have a much broader appeal to project managers in a wide range of industries, who might never have considered it before. As more projects embrace the methods and more knowledge accumulates, new ways will be found to use earned value methods that will, hopefully, mean that project managers will be better equipped than ever to ensure the successful outcome of their projects.

Notes

1. Office of the Secretary of Defense and National Aeronautics and Space Administration (June 1962) *DoD and NASA Guide PERT Cost Systems Design*, p. 17.
2. DODI 7000.2 (1967) *Performance Measurement for Selected Applications*, Department of Defense, Washington DC, 22 December.
3. Ibid., Section 3: Criteria.
4. Ibid.
5. Arthur D. Little Company (1984) *Survey Relating to the Implementation of Cost/Schedule Control Systems Criteria within the Department of Defense and Industry – Phase II*, Department of Defense, Washington DC, 15 August.
6. ANSI website: <www.acq.osd.mil>.
7. Webb, A. J. (1995) 'Integrated Cost and Schedule Control, a survey of UK experience', *Engineering Management Journal*, Vol. 5, No. 3, June.

3 *Terms and Methodology*

All projects consist of a set of activities that lead to the achievement of the project goal. How those activities are performed, who does the work and when they are done should be defined in the project plan. However, there is no absolute requirement for certain types of projects to have a plan – this may be because there is no particular need to complete the tasks in any set order or by any given date, or because later events will be dictated entirely by the results of earlier ones whose outcomes cannot be known with certainty in advance. Where no plan exists, earned value methods are not appropriate and they will not work.

If the project can be seen clearly in terms of 1) the work to be done, 2) the value associated with the work and 3) the order and duration of events, it is possible to generate a time-phased plan and a time-phased statement of the value to be created or the costs to be incurred. At the planning stage, the value to be created and the costs to be incurred can be treated as the same thing; only by spending resources, in terms of cost, is anything of value created. Project plans are typically expressed in the form of a network or a bar (Gantt) chart. Most projects have a start-up phase where a small number of resources are needed, a period of significant activity where the maximum resources are used and finally a winding-down phase as resources are shed and the project concludes. When the cumulative costs associated with these activities are plotted on the basis of time an S-shaped curve will result. The steepness of the slope of the curve represents the level of expenditure; as this is greatest when the project is at peak of activity, the slope of the curve is steepest on or about its centre. Taken together, the planned activities and the costs appear as shown in Figure 3.1

The concept of the earned value

In the period prior to earned value methods, two simple measures of cost on projects were taken: the planned costs and the actual costs. Consider a project with a four-year lifespan with costs that follow an S-curve as shown in Figure 3.1 and budgeted to cost £80m. Now suppose at the end of the second year the cumulative cost is planned to be £40m, providing all the work is done according to plan and at the expected costs. Let us further suppose that at the end of the second year we know from the project accounts that £30m has actually been spent. The picture of this situation would appear as in Figure 3.2.

The question we might now ask ourselves is how well is this project actually doing at the half-way point? On the face of it we might say it is not doing very well, as actual spend is well behind the plan – it could be that the project is behind schedule and we might have cause to worry. On further reflection we might decide that it could be doing very nicely and be completed for a cost that is well below the budget, in which case we might have cause to cheer. Alternatively, we might conclude that it could be either or both these possible scenarios, in which case we really don't know where we are. In fact, it is impossible to tell what the position of the project is with respect to either cost or schedule from these two

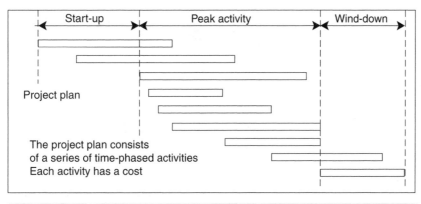

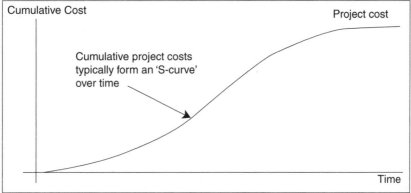

The project plan and the project cost are related in terms of time

Figure 3.1   The relationship between the plan and the costs over time

figures alone. To establish the true position we need two more facts: what have we actually accomplished and what is it worth at the values that we originally put on it when the plans were made? For this we need to go back to the original plan and make an assessment of what has actually been achieved in terms of what was expected when we drew up the plan. If an assessment is made of the actual progress with the activities in the plan, it could appear as in Figure 3.3 where the shading of the bars has been used to represent the degree of completion of each activity at the end of Year 2.

We might now choose to make an assessment of the worth to the project of the achievement so far. If we examine the percentage achievements of all the activities that should have started by the end of Year 2, we might conclude that just over 31 per cent of the total project plan has been achieved. (This can be seen by the relative areas of the shaded to the unshaded portions of the activity bars, on the assumption that the rate of expenditure on all the activities is similar.) Taking 31 per cent of £80m gives a worth to the project of the work completed at the end of Year 2 as £25m. This is the earned value at the project's mid-point.

Now that we have this additional piece of information we can make a precise judgement about the position of the project at our reporting point. The position is shown in Figure 3.4. Looking at Figure 3.4 indicates that the project is actually in a poor position as not only is actual expenditure below that planned but the earned value is even worse. This project is

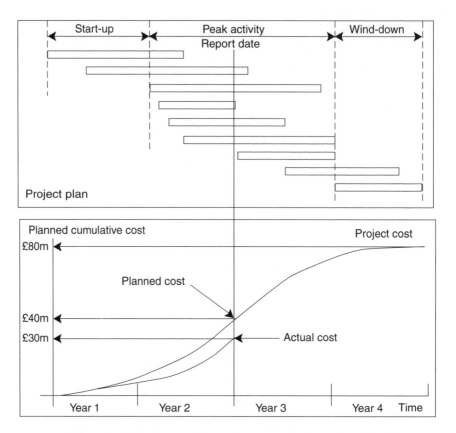

Planned and actual expenditures for a project at the project mid-point

Figure 3.2   Planned and actual expenditure for a project at the mid-point of its life

thus well behind schedule and costing more than was expected for what has actually been achieved. As a project manager, one would certainly not be happy with a situation like that.

Supposing however, our assessment of progress actually looks like that shown in Figure 3.5; here we can see that the shaded area equates to about 56 per cent of the total work content at the reporting date. Fifty-six per cent of £80m is £45m; plotting this point on the cost curves shows that in this case the project is actually doing very well. Not only is work running slightly ahead of schedule but £45m worth of work has been completed for an actual spend of only £30m. If this continues, this project could expect to finish early and at a substantially reduced cost compared to the original estimate.

Calculating the earned value at a reporting point and plotting it against the planned and actual cost curves allows us to see the precise position of the project in terms of both its costs and its progress. This comparatively simple process is the basis of all earned value methods. The important points to note are the fixed relationship between the plan and the costs and the ability to make an accurate assessment of progress. In practice, earned values are calculated regularly throughout the project, not just at the mid-point.

The distinction between the sum that has been spent and the value that has been created or 'earned', as opposed to being planned or scheduled, is the distinctive feature of the

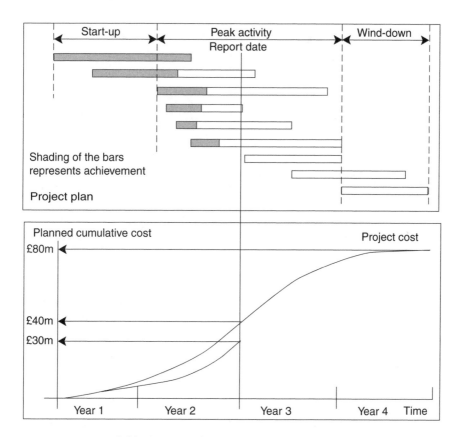

Figure 3.3   Adding an assessment of progress gives further meaning to the project position

approach and leads to the often used titles of 'Earned value costing' or 'Earned value management'. It should however be remembered that the earned value method for project cost reporting was only one feature of the total C/SCSC approach to project control embodied in DoD 7000.2 and implied in the new commercial standard ANSI/EIA-748-1998. The terms 'Earned value' and 'C/SCSC' or 'C-spec' are sometimes used interchangeably but this is wrong. Earned value cost measurement can be applied without incorporating many of the requirements of ANSI/EIA-748-1998.

Earned value terminology

DODI 7000.2 defined a series of terms that have become synonymous with the earned value method of performance estimation. Although they are now common currency, widely used and well understood, there has been a body of opinion that would like to see them changed and other terms used. The original definitions and their associated acronyms are perfectly clear and easy to understand, hence the argument for a change is a weak one; however it does seem to be gaining ground in both the United Kingdom and the USA. The principal motive seems to be to disassociate the earned value principles from its US government origins which

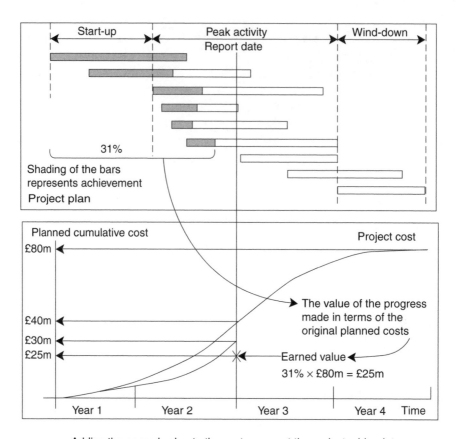

Adding the earned value to the cost curves at the project mid-point

Figure 3.4   The earned value is estimated from the actual achievement based on the original costs

are clearly identified with the standard terminology. As the standard terms are still widely used and are likely to remain in use for the foreseeable future, they will be used here.

It will be realized from the above figures that three measures of cost are required at any reporting point. The standard terms for these three values are:

- **Budgeted Cost for Work Scheduled (BCWS)** (Planned value) – This is the sum of all the planned costs in the project, or any given part of the project, up to the reporting date. (This is the £40m sum in Figure 3.4.)

- **Budgeted Cost for Work Performed (BCWP)** (Earned value) – This is the cost of all the progress achieved on the project, or part of the project, up to the reporting date and expressed in terms of the planned costs originally set out in the initial estimate; it is also called the 'Earned Value' as it represents what has been earned, not simply what has been spent (this is the £25m sum in Figure 3.4). (Chapter 7 gives more details of how the BCWP can be calculated.)

- **Actual Cost of Work Performed (ACWP)** (Actual cost) – This is the total of all expenditure on the project, or part of the project, up to the reporting date; it is the sum of what has

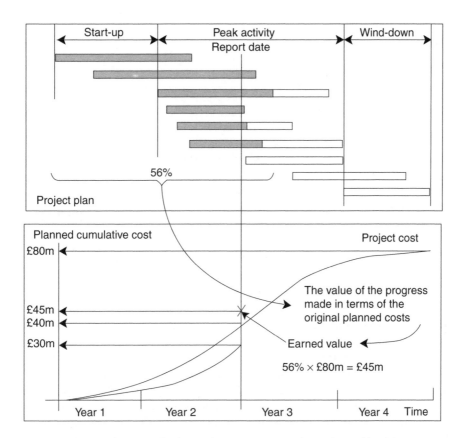

Adding the earned value to the cost curves at the project mid-point

Figure 3.5   Earned value assessment for a project that is running ahead of schedule

actually been spent irrespective of what has been planned or achieved. (This is the £30m sum in Figure 3.4.)

Once the earned value has been plotted, the difference between it and the other two values can be subdivided into that part due to variations in the cost of the work done, that is, the 'Cost Variance', and that part due to work being done at a different time from that scheduled, that is, the 'Schedule Variance'. These variances are shown in Figure 3.6 for the case in Figure 3.4.

From Figure 3.6 it will be seen that:

- **Cost Variance (CV)** = BCWP – ACWP, the numerical difference between the earned value and the actual cost at the reporting point

- **Schedule Variance (SV)** = BCWP – BCWS, the numerical difference between the earned value and the planned expenditure at the reporting point.

Whenever the cost or schedule variances are negative, the project is in a poor position; if the

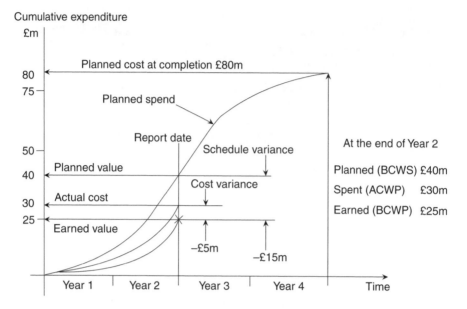

Figure 3.6   Cost and schedule variances

variances are positive then the project is doing better than planned. The separation of cost performance versus schedule peformance is a key benefit of using earned value methods. With projects that do not use earned value methods, accountants take the difference between the planned cost and the actual spend (that is, BCWS – ACWP) to mean the 'Cost Variance' as there is no other variance figure available to them. This is a point that always needs to be remembered.

Cost and schedule variances may be calculated on either cumulative data or periodic (typically monthly) data. These variances should be calculated at the lowest level of detail established within the project and progessively summed through the various levels of the project. This allows the project manager to see where the cost or schedule performance problems are occurring and to take appropriate actions.

Although the Schedule Variance is a calculable number, it may be of less real value than the Cost Variance. However, the Schedule Variance can be turned into a measure of schedule progress by reference to the S-curve as shown in Figure 3.7.

Earned value calculations

Calculation of the Cost and Schedule Variances are the simplest of the earned value calculations but further numerical information can be derived which may be even more helpful. Two useful index numbers can be calculated that give an instant measure of performance against both the cost plan and the schedule. They are defined as:

- **Cost Performance Index - (CPI)** (Cost efficiency) The ratio of the value created to the amount spent at a point in time on the project

$$CPI = \frac{BCWP}{ACWP}$$

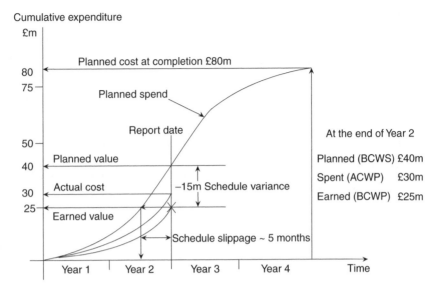

Figure 3.7   Schedule slippage can be established from the earned value and the planned S-curve

- **Schedule Performance Index (SPI)** (Schedule efficiency) – The ratio of the earned value created to the amount of value planned to be created at a point in time on the project

$$SPI = \frac{BCWP}{BCWS}$$

These ratios are shown in Figure 3.8.

Index values greater than one (1) indicate performance either in cost or schedule terms that is better than planned; values lower than one indicate a worse position. The CPI is, perhaps, the more useful of the two, it shows the real worth that is being created by the project, thus a CPI value of 0.85 indicates that for every pound spent, only 85 pence worth of value is being created on the basis of the original budget. The SPI is somewhat more suspect as a measure of progress as it is using money as an analogue of time, which may not be strictly true. Nevertheless, both these performance indices give a valuable clue as to performance to date and what the future may hold.

Over many years of running projects under earned value conditions, it has been evident that trends, once established, tend to remain in force until the end of the project. More depressingly, it has been noticed that if trends do change it is rarely for the better: the situation is far more likely to get worse. Two formulae can be derived for estimating both the expected cost at completion and the expected completion date on the assumption that the trends seen up to the reporting point continue until the end of the project.

For the cost at completion at a reporting point, the formula is made up of two parts: *the cost already expended* plus *the estimate of future cost,* assuming the trends seen to date continue:

- **Estimated Cost At Completion (EAC)** – The estimated final cost of the project is given by:

$$EAC = ACWP + \frac{BAC - BCWP}{CPI} \qquad (3.1)$$

Where: BAC is the Budgeted Cost At Completion

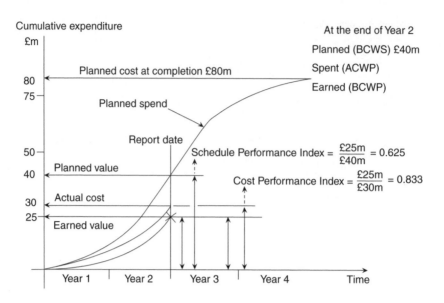

Figure 3.8   The Cost and Schedule Performance Indices

It should be noted that extensive research carried out on hundreds of projects within the USA shows this EAC forecasting method tends to be optimistic; it depends on the same level of cost efficiency to continue to project completion but this rarely happens. More sophisticated formlate are considered later.

For the overall duration of the project the formula also consists of two parts, *the time elapsed up to the reporting date* plus *the estimated additional time to complete the project* assuming the trends seen to date continue.

- **Estimated Time To Completion (ETTC)** – The estimated overall duration of the project is given by:

$$ETTC = ATE + \frac{OD - (ATE \times SPI)}{SPI} \tag{3.2}$$

Where: BAC is the Budgeted Cost At Completion
ATE is the Actual Time Expended
OD is the Original Duration

The calculations using these expressions are shown graphically in Figure 3.9.

It will be seen that a straight line is drawn from the actual spend value to the predicted end conditions. This is because these expressions say nothing about the shape of the cost curve, they are simply point functions and simple linear relationships. In practice the cost curve is likely to be some form of S-curve, but exactly what shape it will take we cannot say from these simple formulae.

Both expressions 3.1 and 3.2 can be reduced algebraically:

Taking the expression for the EAC
To simplify the working, let:

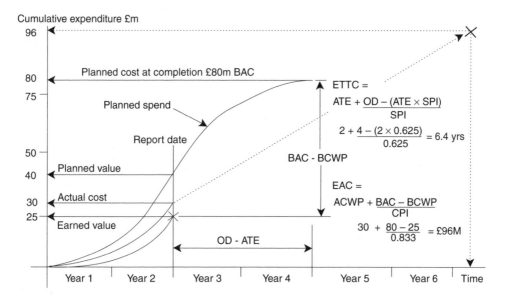

Cumulative expenditure £m

Planned cost at completion £80m BAC

Planned spend

Report date

Planned value

Actual cost

Earned value

ETTC =

$$ATE + \frac{OD - (ATE \times SPI)}{SPI}$$

$$2 + \frac{4 - (2 \times 0.625)}{0.625} = 6.4 \text{ yrs}$$

BAC - BCWP

EAC =

$$ACWP + \frac{BAC - BCWP}{CPI}$$

$$30 + \frac{80 - 25}{0.833} = £96M$$

OD - ATE

Year 1   Year 2   Year 3   Year 4   Year 5   Year 6   Time

Figure 3.9   Calculating the end conditions from the BCWS, BCWP, ACWP, CPI and SPI

ACWP = A
BAC = B
BCWP = P
CPI = C

now: $EAC = A + \dfrac{B - P}{C}$ (3.3)

but $C = \dfrac{P}{A}$ (3.4)

Looking back at expression (3.1):

$$EAC = A + \frac{B - P}{C} = A + \frac{A(B - P)}{P}$$

Bringing to a common denominator:

$$\frac{PA}{P} + \frac{BA - PA}{P}$$

$$= \frac{PA + BA - PA}{P} = \frac{BA}{P}$$

and from expression (3.4)

$$EAC = \frac{B}{C} = \frac{BAC}{CPI} \qquad (3.5)$$

In simple terms, the estimated cost at completion is the original budgeted cost at completion divided by the CPI. This simple formula is often quoted without reference to the more fundamental expression from which it derived.

Looking at the ETTC, the expression is made up of two parts, ATE being the actual time elapsed and the additional part being an estimate of future time based on the current SPI.

Let ATE = T
OD = D
SPI = S
BCWS = W

Now $ETTC = T + \dfrac{D - (T \times S)}{S}$ (3.6)

Looking back at expression (3.6) and bringing to a common denominator:

$$ETTC = \frac{TS + (D - (T \times S))}{S}$$ (3.7)

$$ETTC = \frac{TS + D - TS}{S} = \frac{D}{S} = \frac{OD}{SPI}$$ (3.8)

This algebraic simplification indicates that the ETTC is simply the original planned duration divided by the SPI. However, there are circumstances where this could be misleading; even so, it is the formula that is often quoted. It should be noted that this formula is not normally used within the USA. A more reliable predictor of schedule performance and the end-date can be achieved through analysis of the project plan.

More formulae and performance indices have been devised but the terms, variances and formulae quoted above are probably the most useful. The following worked example will show how they are used.

Case example: Estimate of the outcome of a project at the mid-point of its life

A project set to last seven months contains the eight major tasks with costs and timings shown in Figure 3.10.

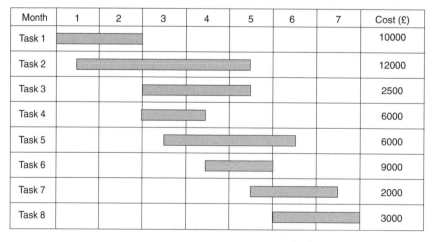

Project task durations, sequences and costs

Figure 3.10   The initial view of the project before work commences

Assuming an even spend rate in each task the expenditure plan is as shown in Table 3.1.

Table 3.1   Expenditure plan

Task	1	2	3	4	5	6	7
1	5000	5000					
2	1500	3000	3000	3000	1500		
3			1000	1000	500		
4			4000	2000			
5			1000	2000	2000	1000	
6				3000	6000		
7					500	1000	500
8						1500	1500
Total £	6500	8000	9000	11000	10500	3500	2000
Cum. £	6500	14500	23500	34500	45000	48500	50500

At the end of Month 3, the position of the project in terms of assessed progress and actual expenditure is given in Table 3.2.

Table 3.2   Position at the end of Month 3

Task No	ACWP £	% Complete
1	9500	100
2	9800	45
3	1200	10
4	1700	15
5	2100	20
Total ACWP	24300	49

Visually this project looks as shown in Figure 3.11.

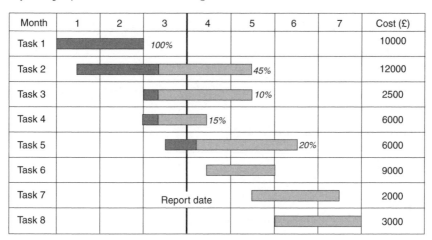

Project progress at the end of Month 3

Figure 3.11   The position of the project at the end of Month 3

To calculate the BCWP, each of the percentage completion figures must be multiplied by the original budgets; this is set out in Table 3.3.

Table 3.3   BCWP calculation at Month 3

Task No.	% Complete	Budget £	BCWP £
1	100	10000	10000
2	45	12000	5400
3	10	2500	250
4	15	6000	900
5	20	6000	1200
Total BCWP	49	36500	17750

Applying the formulae gives the variances, performance indices and an estimate of the project end conditions.

THE VARIANCES

The **Cost Variance** (CV) is: BCWP – ACWP = £17750 – £24300 = –£6550

The **Schedule Variance** (SV) is: BCWP – BCWS = £17750 – £23500 = –£5750

THE PERFORMANCE INDICES

The **Cost Performance Index** (CPI) $= \dfrac{\text{BCWP}}{\text{ACWP}} = \dfrac{£17750}{£24300} = 0.730$

The **Schedule Performance Index** (SPI) $= \dfrac{\text{BCWP}}{\text{BCWS}} = \dfrac{£17750}{£23500} = 0.755$

THE ESTIMATES OF THE PROJECT END CONDITIONS

The **Estimated cost at completion** (EAC)

$$\text{EAC} = \text{ACWP} + \frac{\text{BAC} - \text{BCWP}}{\text{CPI}} = £24300 + \frac{£50500 - £17750}{0.730} = £69163$$

The **Estimated time to completion** (ETTC)

$$\text{ETTC} = \text{ATE} + \frac{\text{OD} - (\text{ATE} \times \text{SPI})}{\text{SPI}}$$

$$= 3 + \frac{7 - (3 \times 0.755)}{0.755} = 9.272 \text{ months from start.}$$

Figure 3.12 shows the position graphically and it illustrates both the potential overspend and slippage that will occur on the basis of the trends to date. It should be noted that the predicted values only indicate the end position; the path in terms of cost versus time by which it gets there is not predicted, although it might be assumed that the path will have a general shape similar to the BCWS curve.

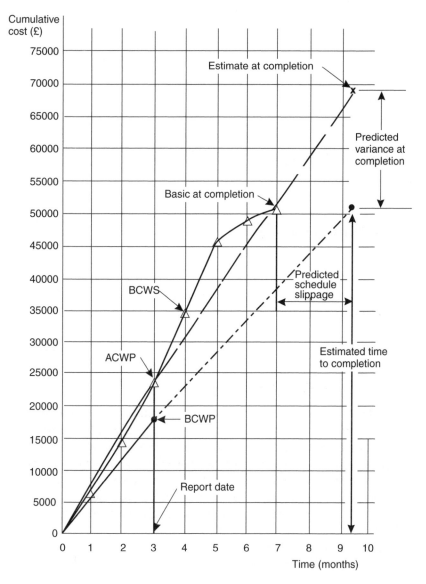

Figure 3.12   Predicted position at project completion based on earned value measurement and formulae

Additional formulae

The formulae used in the above example are probably the most useful, but more values can be calculated if required. Given below is a selection of formulae that are sometimes used to provide additional insight:

- **Variance at completion – (VAC)**

  $$VAC = BAC - EAC \tag{3.9}$$

- **Schedule variance as a percentage of the scheduled achievement – (SV%)**

  $$SV\% = \frac{BCWP - BCWS}{BCWS} \times 100 \tag{3.10}$$

- **Cost variance as a percentage of the earned value – (CV%)**

  $$CV\% = \frac{BCWP - ACWP}{BCWP} \times 100 \tag{3.11}$$

- **% of project schedule to be achieved at the report point**

  $$= \frac{BCWS}{BAC} \times 100 \tag{3.12}$$

- **% complete at the report point**

  $$= \frac{BCWP}{BAC} \times 100 \tag{3.13}$$

- **% spent at the report point**

  $$= \frac{ACWP}{BAC} \times 100 \tag{3.14}$$

- **Other estimates of cost at completion – EAC**

Besides the basic linear formula for the EAC given as expression (3.1), two empirical formulae are sometimes used that take into account the combining effect of both cost and schedule changes. This is saying two things. First, some costs are time-related irrespective of the task content (for example, service activities such as managing the project), when the schedule begins to slip costs will tend to rise as a result of the lengthening of the project and second, if the project is perceived as slipping, additional resources may be deployed, possibly at premium rates, in order to attempt to recover the position thus incurring extra cost.

$$EAC_1 = ACWP + \frac{BAC - BCWP}{(0.5 \times CPI) + (0.5 \times SPI)} \tag{3.15}$$

$$EAC_2 = ACWP + \frac{BAC - BCWP}{CPI \times SPI} \tag{3.16}$$

Formula (3.16) is sometimes quoted as the 'pessimistic' estimate, while others consider it to be the 'most likely' value. Empirical evidence from actual projects would suggest that it is a good predictor of the final outcome and it is often used. It should always be remembered that the most accurate EAC can be calculated by traditional estimating methods through a thorough assessment of hours for remaining work, revised bills of materials and additional project expenses.

- **The 'To-complete Performance Index' for budgeted cost – (TCPI(BAC))**

$$\text{TCPI(BAC)} = \frac{\text{BAC} - \text{BCWP}}{\text{BAC} - \text{ACWP}} \tag{3.17}$$

This formula is used to indicate the level of cost performance that will be necessary to complete the project within budget from the report point.

- **The 'To-complete Performance Index' for schedule – (TCPI(OD))**

$$\text{TCPI(OD)} = \frac{\text{BAC} - \text{BCWP}}{\text{BAC} - \text{BCWS}} \tag{3.18}$$

This formula is used to indicate the level of schedule performance required to finish on time from the report date. In any practical situation, both the To-complete performance indices should be compared with the actual observed performance indices; if there is a significant difference, particularly where much improved performance is required, then the realism of these values must be in doubt.

Table 3.4 shows the calculated values for the additional formulae. Note how much larger the Estimated Cost at Completion is using formula (3.16). This is undoubtedly the reason why it is often dubbed the pessimistic estimate, but why it might also be the most realistic one.

Difficulties with the predictive formulae

Despite the straightforward nature of the predictive formulae, they can lead to difficulties under some circumstances. In some cases the simplified formulae (3.5) and (3.8) are quoted without reference to the original, more fundamental, expressions from which they derive. Whereas the algebra may indicate that this is acceptable, it has a hidden pitfall that particularly affects the calculation of the ETTC. Expression (3.8) states that dividing the OD by the SPI is a correct way to calculate the estimated time to completion; the algebra seems to indicate it, but that conclusion would be misleading. This may not appear obvious, given the working shown, but the explanation lies partly in a quirk of algebra and partly in the nature of what is being done. In essence, cost and time cannot be treated in the same way; when no work is done, costs stand still, but this is not true of time, which goes on whatever the work situation may be. Furthermore, the cost that a project incurs is the sum of all the costs in the project; this is not true of time because the time that a project takes is governed by the time taken by just a few activities, the *Critical* ones. Because of the additive nature of the costs and the fact that the CPI is calculated from the cumulative costs, the EAC expression holds good in its reduced form.

If we look at the SPI, calculated from BCWP/BCWS, we find that it has some rather unusual properties because it is using cost as the analogue of time, which is not strictly true; it works well until the original planned duration is exceeded, after which it changes its character. The schedule aspect of 'Cost/Schedule Control Systems Criteria' has been a problem and there was a debate in the early days as to whether or not the term 'schedule' should be used in the title.

Table 3.4   Earned value calculations using the additional formulae

---

Earned value calculations for the case example

$$
\begin{aligned}
\text{Given} \quad &\text{BCWS} = £23500 \\
&\text{BCWP} = £17750 \\
&\text{ACWP} = £24300 \\
&\text{BAC} \ = £50500 \\
&\text{CPI} \ = 0.73 \\
&\text{SPI} \ = 0.755 \\
&\text{EAC} \ = £69136
\end{aligned}
$$

Variance at Completion

$$\text{VAC} = 50500 - 69136 = £18136$$

Scheduled Variance %

$$\text{SV\%} = \frac{17550 - 23500}{23500} \times 100 = -24.5\%$$

Cost Variance %

$$\text{CV\%} = \frac{17550 - 24300}{17750} \times 100 = -36.9\%$$

% of Schedule

$$= \frac{23550}{50500} \times 100 = 46.5\%$$

% complete

$$= \frac{17750}{50500} \times 100 = 36.1\%$$

% Spent

$$= \frac{24300}{50500} \times 100 = 48.1\%$$

Estimated cost at completion$_1$

$$\text{EAC}_1 = 24300 + \frac{(50500 - 17750)}{(.5 \times .73 + .5 \times .755)} = 68907$$

Estimated cost at completion$_2$

$$\text{EAC}_2 = 24300 + \frac{(50500 - 17750)}{(.73 + .755)} = 83721$$

To-complete performance index (cost)

$$\text{TCPI (BAC)} = \frac{(50500 - 17750)}{(50500 - 24300)} = 1.25$$

To-complete performance index (schedule)

$$\text{TCPI (OD)} = \frac{(50500 - 17750)}{(50500 - 23500)} = 1.21$$

The problem is best illustrated with the following worked example of a project with two major activities with costs and times as shown in Table 3.5.

Table 3.5   Example of the possible error in calculating the Estimated Time to Completion (ETTC)

	Period				
	1	2	3	4	5
The Plan (BCWS)					
Planned Cost, Cumulative £					
Activity A	1000	2000			
Activity B		1000	2000		
Cum. Total (W)	1000	3000	4000		
The Actual Costs Incurred (ACWP)					
Activity A	1000	2000			
Activity B		1000	2000	3000	4000
Cum. Total (A)	1000	3000	4000	5000	6000
The Earned Value (BCWP)					
Activity A	1000	2000			
Activity B		500	1000	1500	2000
Cum. Total (P)	1000	2500	3000	3500	4000
Performance Indices					
CPI (C=P/A)	1.0	0.833	0.75	0.70	0.667
SPI (S=P/W)	1.0	0.833	0.75	0.875	1.000
Estimates at Completion					
EAC (B/C)	4000	4802	5333	5714	6000
ETTC (D/S)	3.0	3.6	4.0	3.4	3.0

Although the EAC shows a steadily increasing prediction in line with the actual costs, there is clearly a problem with calculating the ETTC using the simplified formula as the predicted duration starts to diminish after the planned duration (three periods) has been exceeded. Furthermore, there is an apparent improvement in the SPI from 0.75 at Period 3 to 0.875 at Period 4, even though there is no actual improvement in the rate of schedule progress on activity B which is the only activity current between 3 and 4. The same applies between Periods 4 and 5. This anomaly stems directly from using cost relationships to determine progress through time; in fact, *once the planned duration of any activity or project has been exceeded the SPI becomes a measure of percentage completion, not schedule progress.*

That does not fully explain the reason for the diminishing value for the ETTC and to find it one has to look back at the original expression (3.2). The problem stems from the fact that the algebra says nothing about the relative values of the terms in the expression. Once the duration (D) is exceeded, the whole expression $\left(D - \frac{(T \times S)}{S} \right)$ in formula (3.6) will eventually become a negative value; this is obviously a nonsense as it has the effect of subtracting a sum from the elapsed time and time never goes backwards!

However it can be corrected if it is noted that

$$ETTC = T + \frac{D - (T \times S)}{S}$$

can be used for all cases where the planned duration is not exceeded, that is, $T < D$. Once the originally estimated duration D is exceeded, $T > D$, the formula is changed to:

$$ETTC = T + \frac{T - (T \times S)}{S} \qquad (3.19)$$

that is, the elapsed time is substituted for the original duration.

This can be simplified to

$$ETTC = \frac{T}{S} \qquad (3.20)$$

If this change is made and we look at the situation at Period 4, we now get an ETTC of 4 / 0.875 = 4.57 periods; an improvement on the original and obviously incorrect prediction of 3.4 periods. However, the result could be further improved if the calculation is based solely on the performance of the activity or activities that actually govern the schedule progress of the project. In this case, the reduced form cannot be used and the expression should be modified to:

$$ETTC = T + \frac{D_1 - (T_1 \times S_1)}{S_1} \qquad (3.21)$$

For $T_1 < D_1$
or $D_1 = T_1$ For $T_1 > D_1$
$D_1 \, T_1 \, S_1$ are the values relevant to the critical activity.

In this example, Activity B is clearly critical to progress so it may be decided to generate the ETTC at, say Period 3, using the factors that come from Activity B alone. In this case it will be necessary to calculate the SPI for Activity B at period 3 and it is 1000 / 2000 = 0.5.

Substituting in formula (3.19)

$$ETTC = 3 + \frac{2 - (2 \times 0.5)}{0.5} = 3 + \frac{1}{0.5} = 5 \text{ periods}$$

Using the same formula at Period 4 also gives the correct prediction. In fact, the same procedure of dividing the formula into its component parts could have been applied to the EAC to generate a more precise estimate although this is less important than it is with the ETTC.

The reader is thus left with the choice of using either the simplified formulae if you are happy with the CPI and SPI generated by the aggregate of all costs in the project, or the fundamental formulae if you wish to base predictions on the performance of those current activities which are seen to be critical.

Problems with the SPI result from its use of cost as an analogue of time; however, it is possible to put the time dimension back into the assessment of schedule performance if one has the original BCWS curve plotted over time. By projecting back onto this curve from the

BCWP value from the reporting point, it is possible to measure the achieved progess in terms of time from the start of the project. When this figure is divided by the elapsed time, a measure of schedule performance is derived that is based on the time dimension (horizontal axis) rather than the cost dimension (vertical axis). This method of assessing schedule performance does not suffer from the SPI value always tending towards 1.0 irrespective of actual progress. Figure 3.13 shows the principle. However, it should always be remembered that the best method of determining schedule progress and forecasting the future is to look at the detail of the project plan and see just what is happening on the critical path.

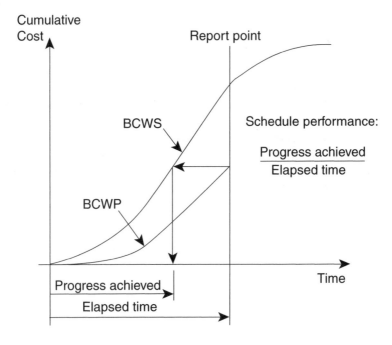

Putting the time dimension back into the
assessment of schedule performance

Figure 3.13   Assessing schedule performance from earned value cost measurements can be improved if the time dimension is put back into the calculation. This removes inherent problems that arise from using cost as an analogue of time and eliminates problems associated with the behaviour of the SPI as conventionally calculated.

Conclusion

The above formulae and worked examples show the basics of all earned value measurements and calculations. It should be noted that many of the features that have become synonymous with the concept of 'earned value management' are absent. None of these calculations makes any mention of a work breakdown structure, a set of control accounts or the organization structure, things which are fundamental features of the C/SCSC approach and which many still consider to the 'correct' method when using earned value management. In fact, none of these things are necessary in order to perform earned value performance measurement at the overall project level. What is needed, however, is a well-thought out and properly costed plan, an accurate and timely cost reporting system and a formal method of assessing progress; all of these features are implied in the worked example. In many real projects, a suitable project management software package is also necessary. From a practical viewpoint, a suitable work breakdown structure is necessary unless the project is very simple and contains few activities. The WBS provides a degree of organization to the plan that makes life simpler from the point of view of data collection and interpretation of the results and outputs.

The simple fact is that earned value performance measurement is an accounting principle, it is not a managerial process at all. The managerial aspect comes from how one sets up the project to obtain the data and what one does with the results that arise.

Earned value was introduced back in the 1960s as part of a much larger and very detailed project management approach and it has not broken free from that heritage. As the worked example shows, earned value performance measurement is something that can be done quite independently of the managerial and work breakdown arrangement whilst it is equally possible to create an organization structure and WBS that follows the C/SCSC approach without doing earned value performance measurement. The two aspects can be treated independently, they are not inextricably linked. The important point is that project managers who wish to use earned value methods do not have to adopt the whole C/SCSC implied methodology; they must learn to choose what parts are most applicable to their project situation and tailor their approach accordingly.

4 *Work Breakdown Structures*

With the advent of formalized project management methodologies in the USA in the 1950s came the idea of the *Work Breakdown Structure* (WBS). This structure was devised to aid Department of Defense civil servants to account for the money that had been spent by the project against the items that had been delivered; the organization of project data in a standard form was made a contractual requirement. Similar accounting structures must have existed in many organizations long before the DoD requirements were written, as it has always been necessary to know how and where money is being spent if control is to be exercised over a business. However, the new formality associated with the work breakdown structure has become firmly woven into the process of project management.

What is a work breakdown structure?

The work breakdown structure (WBS) is, quite simply, a method of identifying and classifying the work content of the project in a rational and easily understood way. Its purpose is to define discrete quantities of work so that:

- They can be uniquely identified for what they are.
- They can be seen for their contribution to the total project.
- They can be monitored and controlled from a time, cost and content standpoint.
- Responsibility for achievement and performance can be allocated.
- Meaningful historic data can be obtained at the end of the project.

All of the above are important from an overall project management standpoint, so creating an appropriate WBS is an essential first step in the handling of any complex project. The WBS is not the same thing as a simple task list although this could specify all the work in the project. Nor is it the same thing as a project plan – which could also be a method for defining all the work in the project. A WBS only specifies work to be done; it does not specify the order in which that work will be carried out as that is a property of the project plan. However, in an integrated project control environment, both the WBS and the plan will need to interface in a harmonious way.

The principal feature of a WBS is a rational arrangement of the tasks that define the work at the lowest level suitable for control; in addition, the arrangement must allow the lower levels to be summarized upwards to broader areas of related activity or responsibility. Some form of coding system that relates to the levels is usually employed for reference purposes. A number of different coding arrangements are possible but they tend to follow one particular aspect of the project such as the product structure, the organization structure or the plan of work, as the chosen aspect is considered particularly important in terms of both reporting and control.

Work breakdown structures used in the past have tended to be product-based and this was encouraged by the US DoD; its contracts define a WBS as a 'product-oriented family tree'. This arrangement helped the DoD's own project managers to account for what their money was being spent on; that is, they could relate expenditure to items of procured hardware or discrete services. The WBS that is imposed under this arrangement is called the 'contract work breakdown structure' as it is specifically designed for reporting against the contract statement-of-work which is normally written in terms of the hardware or other specified services to be delivered. The idea that a WBS should be 'product oriented' has become so embedded in the conventional wisdom of earned value performance measurement and the general principles of project management that some project managers believe it to be either the 'official', 'right' or the 'only' form of WBS. A work breakdown structure has been desribed as:

> ... a product-oriented task hierarchy of all the work to be performed to accomplish the project contractual objectives. The products may be software, hardware, documents, tests, reports, support services or other quantified elements of the objectives ... Use of the term 'product oriented' does not mean ... that the WBS should follow a structural decomposition of the functions of the delivered product unless this is appropriate.

This somewhat ambiguous definition is clearly aimed at a project situation with a contract between a sponsor and a contractor for the work. It is thus designed to conform with a contract that sets out the project in terms of deliverables: components, finished goods, documents and services, for which both prices and time-scales can be determined. This is very much how the US Department of Defense operated, expecting a considerable amount of time and effort to be spent at the start of the project to plan and cost all the activities in detail before contracts were signed. Nevertheless the DoD did expect the WBS to follow the principal physical breakdown of the product because that is how it wanted costs to be reported. Besides the overall project situation, it was interested in the position on each of the major elements of the end product. This is particularly important with a complex product; for example, a combat 'plane is composed of a set of 'systems' such as airframe, radar, engines, guns, etc, each of which is a development project in its own right and which all have to be brought together in the final product. Difficulties with any of these system components could impinge directly on the conclusion of the total project. Cost reporting in that format also allowed the DoD planners to assemble historic data that could be used to estimate and compare the costs associated with developing new items of defence equipment. By knowing the costs and time-scales associated with developing all the various components, new projects could be seen and estimated more clearly at the concept development stage; this clearly placed the DoD in a stronger position when it came to negotiating contracts for new systems.

From the DoD's point of view, this whole approach made considerable sense. Whatever problems operating this way caused for industry, the DoD was not concerned; when the DoD tried telling industry how to manage with PERT/Cost it was dealt a sharp rebuff. As a result industrial managers were left to figure out a way to conform with its particular form of WBS and the reporting requirements it imposed under C/SCSC.

The concept of the work breakdown structure

The WBS is a logical way of describing all the work in a project without considering the order of events. If, for example, we consider a project for someone to build a house and garden to their own requirements, they might decide that the project consists of a set of major tasks:

- Administration – obtaining the land and the necessary permissions plus dealing with all the contractors
- Architecture – getting a set of plans drawn
- Structure – engaging a builder to dig the foundations and put up the walls and roof
- Internal systems – engaging contractors for the internal works
- Landscape and garden – engaging a gardener for the external landscaping.

This simple division recognizes the distinctive nature of each of these broad areas while encompassing all the work to be undertaken; at the very highest level a WBS could look as shown in Figure 4.1

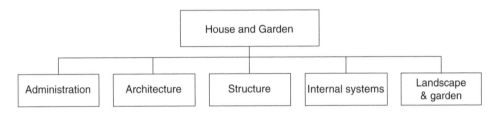

Figure 4.1   Top-level work breakdown structure for a housebuilding project

The top-level WBS serves only to divide the work into identifiable and fairly discrete tasks of different but internally related character. To use the WBS in a meaningful way both for planning and control requires a further breakdown into more detailed aspects that are clearly identifiable as being distinctive. An additional breakdown has been done in Figure 4.2.

At this point it is possible to see all the work in the project in a way that would allow us to 1) plan the project as we can clearly see that some aspects have to be completed before others can start, 2) estimate at a broad level the likely cost of the project, providing we have some data on building costs, and 3) divide the work among the various contractors in a way that suits our purposes and is convenient to the skills available. If, for example, the various aspects are allocated to the contractors in the way that the sponsor has decided that the work should be done, the WBS will look as shown in Figure 4.3.

Note that the allocation of work does not necessarily follow the major divisions of the WBS, although there is some broad grouping. For reasons known to the sponsor, particular tasks have been allocated to particular contractors where there is either a specific preference or one contractor has a skill that is particularly valued – the specially fitted kitchen, for example. This situation is not uncommon, particularly with complex projects.

If necessary, this WBS could be broken down still further into aspects such as labour, material purchases, and services. Thus the work block given as 'foundations' could be further reduced to 1) hire of an excavator, 2) excavation of the foundations, 3) supply of ready-mixed concrete, 4) pouring and levelling of concrete, and 5) disposal of the soil (see Figure 4.4). Each of these is a separately identifiable purchase or task and is the lowest realistic level to which this work block could be reduced. In practice the whole task might only be about three days' work. For anyone managing the building of a house for their own use, such a detailed

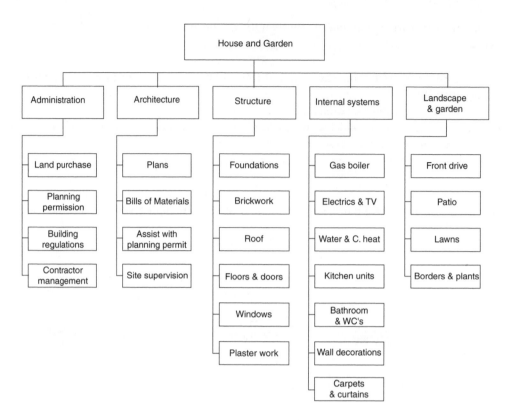

Figure 4.2   Expanded work breakdown structure for a housebuilding project

breakdown would almost certainly not be worthwhile, although the builder might find it worthwhile if he has given a fixed price quote. However, for a developer building an estate of perhaps 100 houses, work estimation at this level would be sensible because of the costs involved; the three days of foundation work on one house turns into 300 days: more than a man-year's work.

Creating a work breakdown structure

For a work breakdown structure to be effective in a practical project situation, four criteria should be met. The WBS must:

1   Impose a rationality upon the project data – there should be a recognized and understood logic to the structure.
2   Contain a hierarchical coding structure – lower levels of data must be capable of being summarized upwards with no loss of accuracy or identity.
3   Compliment existing data gathering systems – the structure must not demand any greater precision, from the data with which it must interface, than can be made available.
4   Conform to the requirements placed upon it – it must allow the generation of appropriate data in a form that is useful.

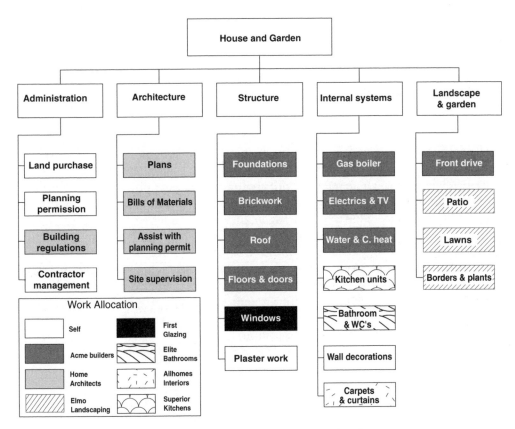

Figure 4.3   Expanded work breakdown structure with allocation of work

Point 1 is self-evident: without it there would be little point to creating a WBS although the structure of the logic can be different depending on requirements. As we have seen from the house-building example, even if a WBS appears logical from one viewpoint it may appear less so when viewed in a different way – by the contractor, for example.

Point 2 follows directly from the logic that is created by observing the rule in Point 1. A work breakdown numbering system is not strictly necessary as work package descriptions or titles could be used, providing one remembers the logic of the structure, but if a computerized or integrated project management system is in use a rational numbering system is essential.

Decimal-based numbering systems are by far the most common and are easily developed and understood. Taking the house-building project a step further, a partial expansion of the WBS is shown in Figure 4.4 with a decimal-based numbering system included. Summing upwards through the various levels of the coding structure will produce aggregate results at successively higher levels; thus the total cost of the Internal Systems – **1.4** is the sum of all the work blocks starting with 1.4, that is, **1.4.1**, **1.4.2**, **1.4.3**, **1.4** etc. However, this WBS arrangement cannot be used to simply determine the value of the work done, for example, by Acme Buildings, the building contractor. The way in which the digits are used represents both the levels of the WBS and the logic of its structure. What each level is taken to represent will depend on how the WBS is to be used and what information is expected to be represented; this has significant implications for the design of the WBS.

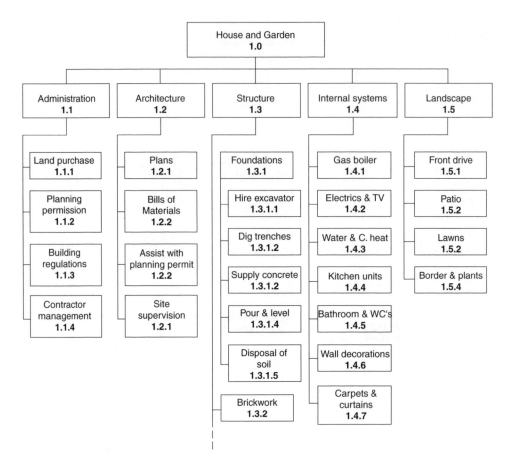

Figure 4.4   Partial work breakdown structure – note expansion of 1.3.1

Points 3 and 4 have practical implications; if they are not met, the whole process of project control could be made difficult, either from a data systems viewpoint or a contractual one. Point 3 states that the WBS coding must fit with the data-gathering systems with which it must interact. With a project like personal house-building, this point may not be significant as the incoming data are all likely to be under direct human control in the form of conversations, letters, invoices, contracts etc, and the information can be extracted and interpreted according to need. With automated systems that are typical of current industry this situation is quite different; costs, times and other information relating to tasks are gathered on computerized systems and normally conform to strict rules as to format and content.

There is no point in defining a WBS coding system that demands levels of subdivision of data that is greater than the basic level at which data is collected by the normal company procedures. For example, if one wishes to collect costs automatically against tasks in the WBS, it would be pointless devising a six-digit code for detailed tasks if the company's time-sheet system (the principal system through which information about what work is being done, by whom and how much) can only cope with five digits. Often these information-gathering systems are fundamental to the company's accounting procedures and, unless the project is very big and of great importance, they are unlikely to be changed. Any project WBS that aims to interact directly with existing company systems must conform to the limitations they impose. In some cases this can cause problems, particularly if a company is in the position of a contractor to a sponsoring company that demands reporting against a WBS that the sponsor has devised for reasons of their own.

Point 4 relates directly to the uses that are expected from the data generated by reporting against the WBS. In the case of the US DoD, it was concerned to gather data about the progress and costs associated with the specific items of deliverable hardware, hence its insistence on the WBS being 'product oriented'. This was the basis of the WBS logic and all the input data was required to support this overall requirement.

If the funding sponsor for a project, be it the US DoD or any other organization, demands cost reporting in a product-oriented format then clearly the WBS must, in one form, conform with that requirement. If, in the house-building example, the principal requirement is to gather and accumulate costs against each of the principal contractors then the WBS format shown in Figures 4.1 to 4.4 would not be the most convenient one.

The product-oriented format is not the only structure possible; when devising the WBS it is for the project organization to consider how it intends to control the project, what data it wishes to use as input to the control process and what data it expects to generate as a meaningful output. A wrong choice of WBS at the start of the project could lead to reporting difficulties when the project gets into full swing.

Many forms of WBS can be devised; each project is likely to be unique, if only in a small way, but they generally conform to one of four basic types:

- product based
- organization based
- task based
- hybrid structures embodying two or three of the above.

Figure 4.5 shows the first three alternatives.

The product or physical structure, Figure 4.5a, gives a costing system that relates costs to the physical elements of the product. Here, when costs are collected, they will show what parts of the product have been worked on and how much has been spent on designing or making each element; what it may not easily tell is who (that is, what department) has been doing the work. In practice, a totally product-based WBS may not be possible as aspects of the project may have an all-embracing character and may involve a service rather than a product; managing the project is one example, while compiling the project accounts is another.

With an organizational structure, illustrated in Figure 4.5b, work is defined according to the department within the company that does the work. When costs are collected through the time-sheet or bookings system, cost reports will show which departments or divisions in the company have been working on the project and how much has been spent in those areas.

The task or functionally based structure, shown in Figure 4.5c, relates costs to the tasks that are expected to be performed. Cost reporting in this arrangement shows what work people have been performing in terms of the tasks they normally carry out. This system might seem to offer less than the other two in terms of control but it has much more to recommend it than either of the others, in the context of integrated earned value per-

a) **Product-based Work Breakdown Structure**

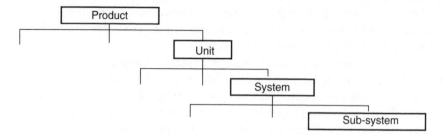

b) **Organization-based Work Breakdown Structure**

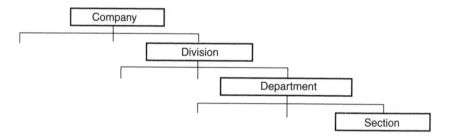

c) **Task-based Work Breakdown Structure**

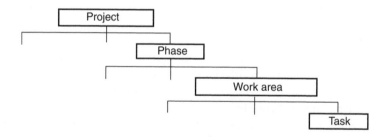

Figure 4.5   Alternative work breakdown structures

formance measurement. The reason is that in order to assess progress it is necessary to refer to the project plan and this is normally structured around the activities or tasks that are expected to be performed. Because the other structures lay their emphasis on either 1) what part of the product is being worked on or 2) who does the work, it is often difficult to construct a satisfactory plan in those formats that fully describes the planner's intentions. Planners think in terms of tasks rather than components or departments, particularly where the work involves bringing together components and where the work is shared across departments.

Hybrid structures can also be constructed that embody elements of two or more of these structures, an example is shown in Figure 4.6.

Each of the levels in the structure gives the information of interest that will be accumulated at the given level. This will be significant for project management and is an important factor in the design of the structure. In practice, such an arrangement might prove difficult to integrate with both the planning system and the cost collection system as it has,

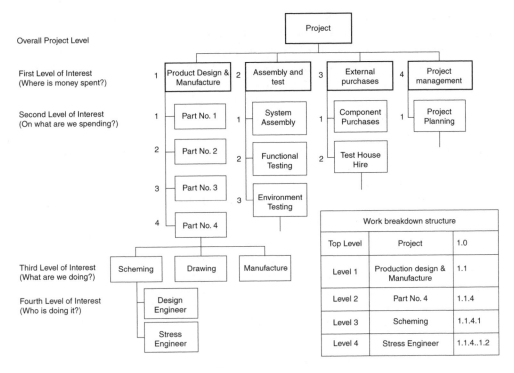

Figure 4.6 Hybrid work breakdown structure showing the different levels of interest and how they are summarized upwards. As the lowest level in this structure is a skill (stress engineer, design engineer, etc.): integrating it with the plan and reporting system may be difficult

Concorde Work Breakdown

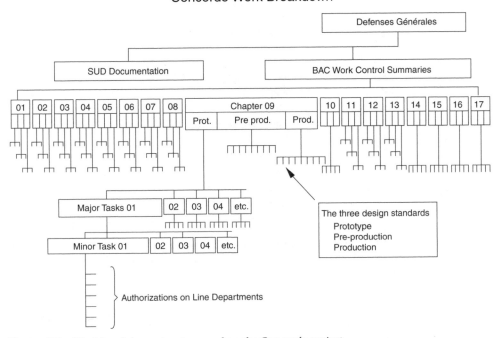

Figure 4.7 Work breakdown structure used on the Concorde project

at its lowest level, the responsible person or required skill. However, integration with the plan would be possible at the third level, that is, the work being done.

Besides providing a rational structure to the project data that will aid both reporting, interpretation and progress measurement, the WBS can form a bridge between the planning system and the company's systems for cost and time reporting, providing it is properly constructed. This is very important in the context of earned value methods, particularly if an integrated approach is required. Work breakdown structures are best devised and implemented at the start of a project.

An example of a WBS that was actually used on a major project is given in Figure 4.7 and Table 4.1. Although this was constructed over 30 years ago, it is basically a task-based structure rather than a product-based one and has, at its lowest level, minor tasks that relate directly to the plan; it is thus a rather more modern approach than the traditional work breakdown structures that have often been advocated.

Table 4.1   Chapter numbers for the main work blocks within the Concorde work breakdown structure. Chapter 9 relates to flight tests which in turn is broken down firstly by the three design standards and then into major and minor tasks as shown in Figure 4.7.

Chapter No	Subject
1	Design
2	Systems Tests
3	Structures Tests
4.1	Wind Tunnel Tests
4.2	Mock-ups and Space Models
5	Simulator
6	Equipment Design and Development
7.1	Tool Design
7.1	Tool Manufacture
8	Aircraft Manufacture
9	Flight Tests
10	Not used
11	Ground Equipment
12	Spares
13	Technical Publications
14.1	PERT
14.2	Liaison and Transport
14.3	Translation and Enquiries
15	Refurbishing
16	Reserve
17	Material and Equipment Stocks
20	Post C of A Development Preparation

Work breakdown structures need care in their construction; a poorly conceived structure will:

- prove difficult to integrate with existing data systems and reporting structures, and
- fail to provide information in a form in which it can be most useful.

The way in which the WBS relates to other data structures in the project is discussed in Chapter 6.

5 *Plans and Budgets*

All earned value techniques rely on a well-conceived project plan. The project work must be clearly perceived at the start and well understood in terms of both what is to be done and the order it should be done. Sometimes these criteria cannot be met; the reasons could be:

- There is an extensive amount of experimentation involved.
- The work is highly innovative with many uncertainties.
- The strategy involves taking advantage of whatever opportunities may arise.
- External forces are likely to dictate the course of the project.

With situations such as those given above, it is very difficult to plan any project with confidence that the plan will remain firm and workable over anything but the shortest horizon. Projects with these characteristics tend to be hostages to fortune; they could make very rapid progress if things fall into place but equally they could be subject to delays, overruns and major changes of direction and may even end in cancellation. This is not to say that such projects are not worth starting: some may make a significant breakthrough that could result in a major competitive advantage. What must be recognized is that projects which cannot be planned with reasonable certainty contain significant risks. Projects of this type might be described as 'entrepreneurial' or 'radical' in character; earned value methods were not designed to handle such projects.

Earned value performance measurement may be a project accounting technique but its origins lay in a contractual arrangement between a sponsor and a contracting organization. In particular, the sponsor wished to have assurance that what has been contracted for will be carried out in line with an approved schedule of activities and within an approved budget. If variances arose, the sponsor wanted to be able to see where those variances were occurring and be able to estimate what the overall effect on the project was likely to be. So, earned value methods started as a form of assurance that projects were understood in sufficient depth, planned in sufficient detail and controlled in such a way that a contract could be agreed between both parties that had a reasonable chance of being fulfilled in line with the original expectations. A contractual arrangement is not, however, a requirement for earned value methods as they could be used equally well on an in-house or private venture project. What is important is that the project is understood and planned to a degree that would be suitable for a contract to exist. However, the existence of a contract is not a guarantee that a project will be planned to the degree that it deserves and this fact undoubtedly accounts for some of the well-publicized project disappointments.

Planning and the project cycle

The principal steps in the project life cycle are given in Figure 5.1; for convenience, the cycle has been divided into five major blocks. The execution and control blocks are so interlinked that they could be considered as one but, as they represent different functions, they can be treated separately.

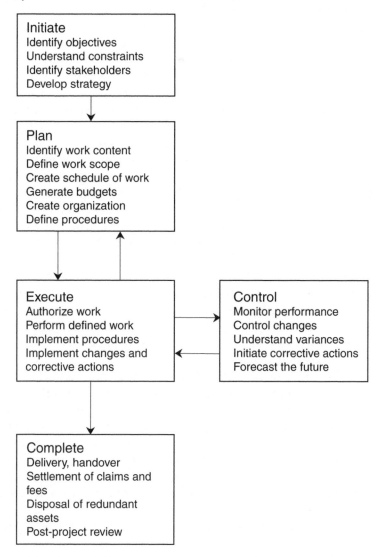

Figure 5.1   The project cycle of activities

All projects start with some form of initiation phase where the ideas for the project are first discussed. Projects are started for a host of reasons but they all have one thing in common: the sponsor or initiator expects to gain some form of benefit from a successful conclusion. These benefits may be seen as the objectives of the projects; if they are not achieved, the project will be worthless. However, the realities of the world in which the project exists can have a major bearing on the form of the project, which could include such things as the likelihood of achieving the objectives and the constraints that are placed on what can be done. The process of initiation should conclude with the development of the project strategy, that is, the overriding set of decisions that will shape all that follows. Strategic matters could involve fundamental decisions regarding what will be done in-house and what will be outsourced, what risk-sharing arrangements will be put in place, what partners to seek and what organization will be set up. In some cases these may be simple decisions because the project is small and straightforward or because there is a successful precedent for doing things a particular way, but in other cases these could be major decisions that have a fundamental bearing on what project structure is created and how the project is conducted.

Planning for the project must be carried out within the strategic framework. For some organizations, such as contractors, who are told what is expected of them, project strategy may not be a major issue. Even so, contractors are often advised only of the requirements: how they achieve them is up to them, but to convince the sponsor they are the right contractor to employ, they may have to produce a credible plan.

Planning involves identifying the work to be done. This can rarely be done in detail at the start as not enough information will be available. However, a start has to be made and the most useful starting-point is to rationalize the work into identifiable and discrete major blocks of work. The process of doing this has already been described in Chapter 4, on work breakdown structures. A work breakdown structure is not a plan as it does not define the order of working; earned value methods imply the control of both cost and schedule and the schedule aspect is absent from the WBS.

For the purposes of control, all planned activities require a 'scope of work' to be defined – this is quite simply a statement of what is included in the activity and, by exclusion, what is not. At the highest level of the project, the scope of work could be fundamental to what is included in the contract between the parties, while at much lower levels it could be simply a definition of an activity. Nevertheless, without a clearly understood scope of work no one can be sure what is expected from any activity.

A definition of work to be done through a host of activities will not form a plan unless it shows how the work is to be done, in particular, the order in which the activities must be performed. Unless it consists of a set of unrelated activities, no project can be performed in random order; with most real projects there is often a very clear basic order that is evident from the nature of the project and it cannot be avoided. Nevertheless, there are usually choices about the way individual activities are performed and how they relate to other dependent activities. Positioning activities in relation to one another and placing them in their correct position in time is the essence of the planning process, it is fundamental to effective project management and to the use of earned value methods. To be useful, the planning must be done in sufficient detail that discrete activities can be identified at a level that can 1) be used for direct control, and 2) be related to other activities so as to accurately define the whole programme of work. There are some obvious difficulties with this that relate directly to our own abilities to perceive accurately all that is necessary and all that will occur. The larger and more complex the project and the greater the span of time over which it is conducted, the more difficult this becomes. This problem is recognized in the concept of 'rolling wave planning' which expects activities in the near term to be planned in detail while activities that recede further into the future are planned in progressively broader blocks.

All activities require resources of one sort or another – these could be materials, labour, services or facilities. The notional allocation of resources to the activities shown in the plan is often termed 'resource scheduling'. It may be the case that allocating resources to the plan as originally set out will show resource demands that cannot be met. This will call for a revision of the plan to conform with the resource constraints. When the schedule of activities is made compatible with the available resources the project will have a viable plan, assuming there are no unforeseen elements that could make it impossible to complete some activities on time. All resources have a cost, whether it is direct payments for materials, services and facilities or charges for labour and the associated overheads. When resources have been scheduled against activities in the plan, costs can be estimated for each activity. Summing all the activity costs in the plan will lead to an overall project cost. Projects contain a degree of uncertainty that is inevitable in anything that attempts to look into the future and do something that has not been done before. It is therefore normal to include a contingency for costs associated with unforeseen work and events that may occur but are not included in the plan. The addition of a contingency to a basic identified cost for an activity creates a 'budget' – a sum of money which it is expected will cover the cost of the activity when the work is performed. Summing all the budgets plus any overall contingency will generate the initial project budget; this is often termed the 'baseline' position, that is, the initial starting-point from which all progress will be measured. This initial planning process is illustrated in Figure 5.2.

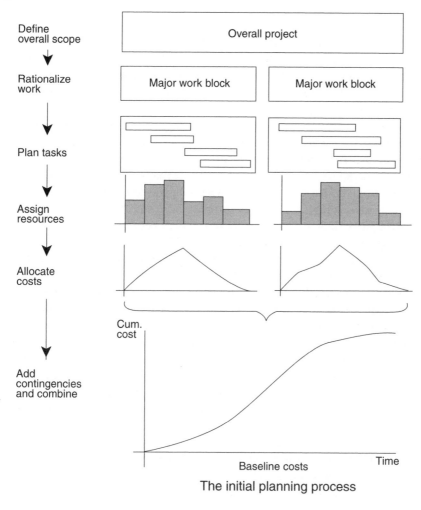

The initial planning process

Figure 5.2   Generating an initial plan for both activities and costs

For contemporary projects of any size, the planning and budgeting process will be done using a software package that contains network drawing and analysis, resource scheduling and activity costing. Compared to the position of 15 years ago, things are very much easier for the project planner and a great deal of drudgery has been removed; nevertheless the amount of thought and attention to detail has not been lessened. If anything, modern methods require much greater discipline as the element of discretion does not exist in integrated, automated systems. More information on current packages is given in Chapter 8.

The work content of the project, the plan of work, the schedule of resources and the set of budgets form the basic set of information that any project needs if it is to go forward in an orderly way, but information is not the only thing a project requires. All projects must have an organization structure and a set of rules and procedures by which it must operate. Decisions about these important aspects are required at the planning stage – it is too late to leave it until the project gets going.

Baselines

The project baseline is an essential feature of any project performance measurement system; if the project started from a position that was known to be incomplete or unclear then attempts to measure, as opposed to simply observe, progress are always going to be suspect. Baseline plans take time to compile in the detail required – for some very large projects, periods in excess of one year might be required with a great deal of thought and discussion with all the parties. It is at this stage that projects attempting to use earned value, particularly in the United Kingdom, have gone wrong; quite simply, far too little time has been spent on developing the baseline plan in the degree of detail required. This in turn has arisen from the practice of putting work out to competitive tender with, perhaps, a 12-week period in which to respond with the fully costed plan and then awarding the contract on the basis of the lowest price. If the work is complex there may not have been sufficient time to develop the plan fully; when the work starts the deficiencies in the plan become apparent and changes must be made which then makes reporting difficult against the original plan. This can be made worse if the contract is let on a fixed-price basis; however, in this situation the contractor may not be willing to provide anything more than BCWP data.

Earned value methods were developed in the 1960s when cost-plus-fee contracting was the normal arrangement for large defence procurement contracts, as this reflected the inherent uncertainty in this type of work. The US Department of Defense recognized that the time taken to submit a tender might be too short to develop an accurate baseline plan so it allowed a period after contract award where further work on the plan could be done before the baseline was finally established. It was accepted by the DoD following the Arthur D. Little study, that with large projects 18 months might be needed before a baseline programme could be agreed. This fact alone could mean that significant changes could be introduced into the plan submitted at tender award in the light of more detailed study. It also tends to emphasize the point that earned value methods were intended for use in a cost-plus-fee contractual arrangement. Both these points have been overlooked, or were never understood, when some projects have attempted to use earned value methods; inevitably they have run into reporting and measurement difficulties.

Budgets and contingencies

All plans and budgets for projects are, to a some extent, estimates of what will happen. Estimates imply a degree of uncertainty, they are not a guarantee and they could be wrong. It is beyond the scope of this text to go into the reasons why estimates turn out to be wrong or the many methods that have been devised for generating estimates for project work but techniques include:

- subjective estimating, based on experience and intuition
- synthetic estimating, based on a build-up of known measurable elements (synthetics)
- comparative estimating, based on a rational comparison with previous projects
- parametric estimating, based on formulae and key project characteristics (parameters).

Whichever methods are used there will still be an element of uncertainty, and the greater the degree of novelty or innovation the greater the uncertainty. Resolving issues of uncertainty that arise in the course of the project generally involves expending more effort and resources and they could also require more time than was originally conceived. It is therefore normal to add a contingency to cover costs, and possibly time, that may be needed to address uncertain issues that could occur.

Company pressures towards underestimation can be considerable. Whether the project is an in-house one or the subject of competitive tendering, there may appear to be advantages in a low initial estimate. All project managers know that a low-cost figure is more likely to gain board-level approval and, in general, is more likely to win in a competitive situation. Another view that is often taken is that if a low initial budget is set, a lower overall project cost will result than if a higher and more reasonable figure had been fixed. Some managers adopt a hard line on estimates, saying they should all be based on success first time and that contingencies should never be included as once they are known people will use them whether needed or not. This attitude may stem from:

- Wishful thinking: 'If I say it will happen, it will happen.'
- A mistrust of human nature, possibly based on experience or an attitude to life in general.

Neither of these show an enlightened attitude, as contingencies represent a reserve to cover the unknown and unforeseen; to refuse to admit contingencies is to assume perfect knowledge of the future.

Of course, there could be good reasons for tendering with a low price but if it is done in the full knowledge that costs may rise and a loss may be incurred, it can be a rational decision aimed at generating business. This is quite a different situation to a low price being generated through internal company pressure that simply distorts judgement.

Some organizations adopt a more reasoned view of contingencies and include a structured build-up within the project budget; Figure 5.3 illustrates this principle. Individual task budgets are set at a level that, in the view of the estimator and the manager responsible for the task, is reasonable for the defined work. This will be the budget issued to the personnel required to perform the task. Several minor tasks can come together to form a major task or work package and, by either a rule-of-thumb or a risk assessment, a contingency is added to the budget to cover underestimates due to unforeseen difficulties in all the minor tasks. The work package manager may, in theory, control the use of contingency to accommodate any overruns.

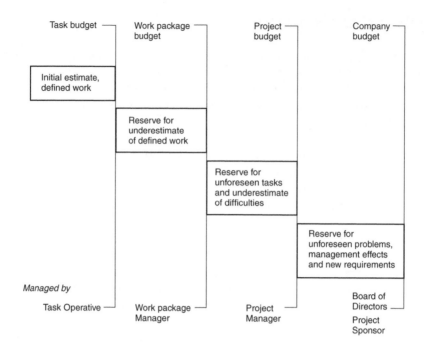

Figure 5.3   Build-up and allocation of contingency to various budgets as used on some UK projects

All work package budgets, including their contingencies, can be summed to give a total budget; to this can be added an overall project contingency which is under the direct control of the project manager and can be released to the work package managers as needed. In the case of an internal project, the company directors can determine the company budget by adding another contingency which can only be released on application to the board by the project manager. With externally sponsored projects, the sponsors can set their own contingency fund to cover contractor cost overruns or additions to the project plan that they may authorize. Whether it is an internally funded or an externally sponsored project, there is no requirement to divulge the size of this contingency to the project manager – it may be wise to keep this matter quiet.

Just how easy it is to 'manage' a contingency fund must be questionable; once a task hits a significant problem and starts overspending, money may have to be spent until the problem is solved, whatever the size of the contingency. Despite this drawback there are merits in this approach:

- It recognizes that the future contains unknowns and if problems arise they are likely to cause project costs to rise.
- Provision is made in the overall company plans for increases in project cost.
- Allocation of the contingency fund to specific tasks gives early warning of potential overspends.

The above arrangement of contingencies, or something similar, is widely used in project work and DODI 7000.2 sought to formalize a slightly different arrangement with specific terms. Illustrated in Figure 5.4, these terms have become synonymous with the earned value

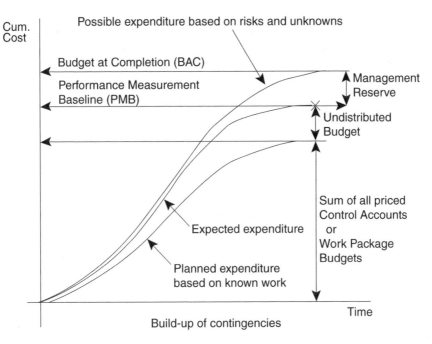

Figure 5.4   Allocation of contingencies and budgets from DODI 7000.2. This approach is implied in ANSI/EIA-748-1998 and is thus the accepted US practice

approach in the USA but they are not so familiar in the UK and, if the work is being done on an internal project where there is no external sponsor, they are not entirely appropriate.

The position is shown in Figure 5.4; unlike the British practice from the early days of C/SCSC until the EVMS standard of today, US practice typically holds contingencies at the project level. This contingency is known as management reserve, and is held and controlled by the project manager for allocation to additional work effort that is still within the scope of the contract. Management reserve should not be allowed to cover or mask cost overruns. The undistributed budget is simply a holding account where the budget for recent contract changes may be held until detailed planning can be accomplished. As the work and budgets are planned in detail, the allocated costs are removed from this holding account. The combination of the existing baseline plus undistributed budget is known as the Performance Measurement Baseline (PMB). An important distinction between management reserve and undistributed buddget is that the latter is for known work, whilst management reseve is held for unknown work. Thus, management reserve is excluded from the PMB. However, the Budget at Completion (BAC) includes the management reserve and is thus the current estimate of the likely overall cost based on an assessment of risks. As the project progresses, some risks will materialize and demand additional expenditure, hence the PMB will move towards the BAC.

Even more confusing can be the question of profits and how to deal with them. This is not an issue if the project is a purely internal affair but it can be important when the project is being undertaken by a contractor. It need not be an issue if work is procured on a simple time-and-materials basis where the appropriate profit is included in the agreed rates. In a cost-plus-fee situation, however, profit is taken by adding a sum to the actual expenditure; the amount will be governed by whatever formula is agreed between the sponsor and the contractor. In the USA, profits are always excluded from performance budgets. This element must be taken into account when the sponsor fixes his final budget; however, the amount of profit paid to the contractor will be set by the actual out-turn costs, which could be more or less than the full budget amount. Furthermore, the profit actually claimed can be influenced by any incentive included in the contract that awards a higher percentage profit if the task is completed at a cost below the planned budget or caps the profit if the cost budget is exceeded. One must be very careful when it comes to incentives, particularly when the performance of the deliverable article or system is also a factor in the profit calculation; it may not be possible to calculate an incentive profit payment (or reduction) until some way into the project and after many activities are complete and paid for. It is also perfectly possible that some activities, materials or services can be procured at fixed prices with profits included.

Earned value, it should be remembered, is an accounting convention for performance measurement; as such it is a project management tool, it is not a profit-and-loss accounting system for a project as a business venture. For this reason it is up to the project sponsor and contractors to agree the budgeting and costing arrangement they intend to use for earned value performance measurement. If profits cannot be simply assessed it would be better to leave them out of the earned value process and perform all the measurements and calculations on the basis of costs alone. Separate provisions will then have to be made in the contractors' and the sponsor's project accounts, both for claiming and paying profits.

At the end of the planning and costing process a plan defining all the activities and their associated budgets will be generated for Board or customer approval, but it is at the Board's approval stage that things can start to go wrong. The plan may look reasonable and the project desirable, but in the eyes of the Board the costs are seen to be too great. Perhaps there is a fear that the competition may be offering something cheaper, that the customer may reject the proposal or that there is not enough money in the company budget for the given year. Sometimes it can come from the customer who may feel that only one contractor has the proper capability to do the required work but the tendered costs are too high. All too often senior management, either on the company or the customer side, concludes that the estimate itself must be wrong. Clearly, they reason, the planners and managers have put in excessive contingencies, made pessimistic assumptions and this time there will not be the problems that occurred on the last project. As most of the estimates represent the judgement of the individuals, they can usually be 'persuaded' by zealous Board members to modify that judgement to something more acceptable. After downward revisions, contingencies are usually the next thing to go; they may be seen as a luxury provision for something that may never happen and if they are included they will be spent whether needed or not. Finally, arbitrary cuts may be applied to bring the budget down to an 'acceptable' level. This depressing story will be only too familiar to many project managers.

Of course, estimates should always be scrutinized and challenged if they seem unreasonable, but one should be careful that scrutiny combined with wishful thinking does not lead to distorted judgement. History shows that the 'savings' made on paper are likely to be illusory and will disappear as the project proceeds. Few development projects are completed within their budgets and most overrun their targets, sometimes by quite massive amounts. This may not necessarily imply a lack of control but simply the impossibility of foreseeing all that will happen in the future and the problems that may be encountered. Project managers should guard against applying wishful thinking and undue pressure for low estimates in an attempt to get their project selected and should be wary if they observe the process in other more senior individuals. An overly optimistic view at the beginning combined with budgets below the real needs of the project can sow the seeds from which really thorny problems can grow later on.

A budget can be considered as a formalized statement of the amount of money provisioned for some activity or purchase. It should, at least at the start, be seen by all parties as adequate to cover the intended work. Budgets should be allocated to members of the project staff charged with directing activities for which they are responsible. Budget allocation may be hierarchical with work package, or control account, budgets being held at a section-head level while lower-level task budgets are delegated to reporting staff who are more directly involved with the work. When a budget is authorized by the project manager, the budget holder is free to spend the sums on the tasks for which he or she has responsibility and are contained in the approved project plan. With a properly controlled project, it should not be possible to start spending on activities that have not been authorized.

6 Data Structures and Reporting Relationships

The previous chapters have dealt with the information and calculation aspects of earned value methods without reference to the organization structure in which they must operate and the other information systems with which they must interact. To understand how earned value methods were intended to operate within a company we need to return to the original US Department of Defense's Cost/Schedule Control Systems Criteria (C/SCSC) specification, what it had to say has generated a legacy that is still with us.

The fundamental data structure

Besides the work breakdown structure (WBS) discussed in Chapter 4, the implementation guide to the DoD's Cost/Schedule Control Systems Criteria (C/SCSC) procedure went on to define the 'organization' as a structure that reflects the way the contractor has organized his people for both responsibility and reporting. When this structure is laid out as a hierarchical arrangement it is often and quite sensibly referred to as the '**Organization Breakdown Structure**' (OBS) although these words were not actually used in the original document. Furthermore, the C/SCSC implementation guide sets out a fixed relationship between the OBS and the WBS; where these two structures meet – that is, where a package of identifiable work can be associated with a responsible part of the organization – a **control account** is created (this was formerly known as a 'cost account' and is sometimes still referred to as such, particularly with some software packages). This relationship is shown in Figure 6.1; the array of control accounts is called the **Responsibility Assignment Matrix** (RAM). This fixed relationship was fundamental to the way in which the C/SCSC procedure was intended to work, and is mandatory when some specialist earned value software packages are used, again reflecting how some aspects of earned value have become dominated by this initial US approach.

The significance of the control account as the principal means of cost collection has not really been appreciated in the UK and the term is little used; much more stress is laid on the WBS for cost collection. As for the project schedule, this was normally contained within a network but, due to the failure of PERT/Cost, the DoD did not insist on the use of networks for project planning and some contractors avoided using them. However, given the abundance of cheap and effective project management software, that approach is now antiquated, as all contemporary software makes use of a network as the principal data model for the project even though a Gantt chart may be the preferred form of display.

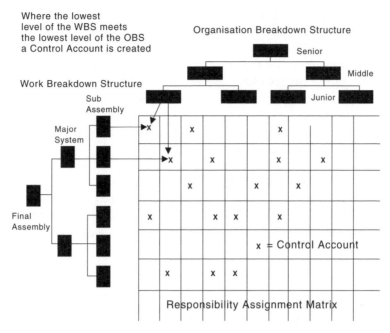

Figure 6.1   Organization structure for C/SCSC reporting according to the US Department of Defense in DODI 7000.2.

Whereas the relationship shown in Figure 6.1 is easy to comprehend at a high level and thus reasonably easy to construct, things can get a lot more complicated when the schedule or project plan must be included in the data structure. The US DoD sidestepped this issue, possibly because it recognized the difficulties, and simply left it to individual contractors to find a way through these complications.

Increased complexity

It must be recognized that it is a major complication for any project control system to use earned value methods compared to a reporting system that does not use them. The reason for this is that to use earned value methods, both the timing of events and the degree of progress must be input into the project data system in a coordinated manner. However, this precise coordination is not an absolute requirement for a project reporting system. For example, it is quite simple to devise an elementary work breakdown structure, perhaps dividing the project into a few major work blocks – admin, design, manufacturing, etc. – and asking all staff to book their time and record their purchases against these blocks. At any reporting point, costs can be accumulated for each block so that actual cost-to-date against total budget can be seen, but there is no measure of value created. Likewise, it may be relatively simple to draw a project plan in Gantt chart or network form and use it both to indicate the work to be done and mark it up with progress as it is observed. This is an uncoordinated arrangement as the plan and the WBS need not bear a rigid relationship to one another other than that they both relate to the same project – this is the simplest system of all.

With the uncoordinated arrangement, staff in, for example, the manufacturing area may book their time to the manufacturing work block for the given project but what specific work they have been doing is not recorded. For small, short-duration or relatively simple projects this may be all that would be needed; the general overview given by the cost report and the marked-up schedule should give the project manager the visibility necessary for high-level control. Day-to-day direction, on the other hand, requires much closer control than would be possible through the time-booking and accounting system which, if it operates on a monthly cycle, might not produce data until six weeks after some of the work is done. Despite the relative simplicity of this reporting arrangement, it need not imply a lack of overall control as formalized change requests and approved budget revisions can still be applied to ensure that unapproved work does not get into the plan and approved changes are formally recognized. Many organizations operate in this way satisfactorily; until the advent of earned value methods the uncoordinated approach was the norm.

When companies first began applying earned value methods, little thought was given to the relationship between the plan and the WBS and, in consequence, the technique proved awkward to apply; the reason is given in Figure 6.2. In theory, each control account should

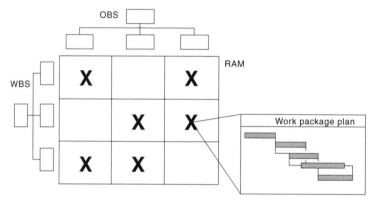

The theory: each control account translates into a work package plan.

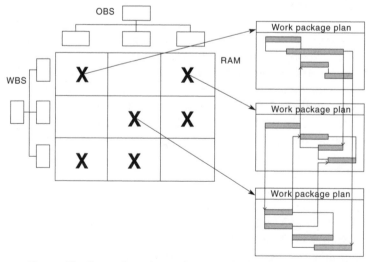

The reality: the work package plans may be intimately interlinked.

Figure 6.2   Simple expansion of the Control Accounts in the RAM can lead to a complex relationship between the basic data structure and the project plan

translate into a major work package which can then be planned for its detailed tasks. As one aspect of the control account is the organization structure, this tended to generate major work packages that related to skills, jobs or departments. However, in many tasks, people from different departments were expected to work together or in a strict sequence so the plan actually contained a complex series of links between each of the major work packages. This underlying complexity is not apparent in the basic WBS/OBS/RAM structure. This, in itself, is not a problem until things start to change; when this occurs changes in one area can permeate through the plan causing changes throughout. This inevitably has implications for the reporting baseline as it no longer reflects the intention of the project.

This difficulty was ignored by the DoD who simply demanded that industry find a way to make their imposed idea of a fixed relationship between the WBS, OBS and RAM work in the context of an earned value reporting system. Difficult though it may have been, this was not impossible as the project plan was in the hands of the planners whose job it was to monitor the situation and make an assessment of progress, whilst the costs were in the domain of the accountants who can normally provide the up-to-date expenditure. In the early days these two sets of data were not necessarily coordinated and they certainly were not integrated, as no suitable software existed to do the integration. Things got really difficult when the plan existed in several different forms; this can happen when some part of the project cannot be satisfactorily handled by a network and has to be dealt with another way. An example of this can occur if the project includes a major manufacturing effort that requires items to be made in varying standards and in large numbers (for example, weapons development projects). In this case the whole manufacturing plan might be handled by a Manufacturing Resource Planning (MRP) production control type of system and separated from the network-based plan.

Despite the problems, by some means, progress and value of work done was agreed between the planners and the accountants and a measure of performance derived. This was set against the baseline plan and used for reporting to the customer. A consequence of this was the advent of two plans: a customer, baseline plan for reporting purposes, and a current or internal plan that reflected the latest thinking and to which people were expected to work.

Despite all the advances in project management methodology, with a project that is beset with frequent changes and is also the subject of a formalized contractual arrangement between the parties, it is difficult to avoid ending up with two sets of plans. A look at the earned value website note-board will show that more than thirty years after EV was implemented this is still a subject of debate (see <www.acq.osd.mil/pm/>). It probably never will be fully resolved, as there is a fundamental incompatibility between the notion of reporting against a plan which reflects the original thinking and asking people to work to the latest instructions which will inevitably be based on knowledge gained since the original plan was created. Some project managers have actually tried to run projects for long periods without allowing any changes or updates to the plan, even when deviations occur. This can work if the project generally proceeds according to the plan and deviations are minor, but if there are serious deviations, failure to update the plan with the latest thinking simply leads to confusion and lack of direction. Other companies have formalized the two-plan arrangement by openly admitting to a 'customer programme' for reporting to the sponsor while having a 'company programme' which reflects the current plan to which staff are working. Often the customer programme has both time and cost contingencies included which are not in the company programme (either as a kind of incentive to the team or a deliberate management reserve), although it is generally assumed that these will be consumed in the course of the project. The inevitable double book-keeping involved in this approach leads to a lot of bureaucracy. Whether such a method is used is likely to depend on 1) the attitude of the sponsor regarding the degree to which he demands reporting against a fixed, immutable baseline plan, and 2) how well perceived at the outset is the plan and the likely level of changes.

Integrated systems

Although earned value systems are now advocated as a method for general project control at all levels, it should be remembered that it was originally advocated by an external sponsor, the DoD, who wished to have both overall project information and detail where it was needed about general progress in terms of cost and schedule. In short, the sponsor wanted a clear and unequivocal view of exactly what the overall cost and schedule progress was in terms that could not be disguised by the contractor. The sponsor was not, however, interested in exercising day-to-day control. But, by imposing a series of operating criteria upon the contractor, which were considered to be good management practice, the DoD hoped to ensure that proper day-to-day control was applied, though not necessarily through the earned value aspect alone.

The demands of reporting against a baseline plan combined with the lack of suitable software to integrate both the plan and the costs meant that, in the early days, earned value reporting was done largely for the benefit of the sponsor; in the case of the DoD, it was a service for which it was willing to pay the extra costs. Day-to-day control was carried on by other means but both the project (program) manager and the sponsor were interested in the earned value reports, as they clearly showed the overall project position and highlighted areas where things were not going to plan. It must be said, however, that the difficult areas were often clearly perceived and may well have been openly discussed well before the earned value reports came out! Nevertheless the overall trend information was useful to both parties.

A principal reason why the DoD imposed earned value methods on its contractors was for the visibility of cost and schedule progress that EV generated; this may well have been more important than any improvements in performance that came through the managerial demands of the C/SCSC. This visibility is very useful when a multitude of defence projects are proceeding simultaneously with each making different levels of progress. Being able to forecast the likely progress of a variety of projects over a period of several years ahead is hugely valuable when it comes to planning future actions and budgeting for cash in future years; furthermore it can avoid the embarrassment of having to go back to the government for more funds due to unforeseen situations arising that could, with more foresight, have been anticipated. For example, if clear slippages are being foreseen for the in-service date of a new fighter aircraft, this has far more implications than for just the new fighter project alone. Existing aircraft will have to be maintained in service for a longer period involving additional and as yet unbudgeted maintenance costs, which could be large if the planes are nearing the ends of their design lives and supporting programmes such as pilot training might have to be put back. Knowledge based on reliable forecasts is of great value when it comes to decision making; decisions such as those associated with retaining older aircraft in service might have to be taken well in advance of the conclusion of the main project, as you simply cannot afford to wait until the end to see what happens. With earned value reporting and the associated forecasting, the DoD could practise a form of 'portfolio management' of its many projects with greater ease and certainty than before. By having a better view of what is likely to happen in the longer term across a range of projects, the DoD could make better decisions about what actions to take in the short term about individual projects and others that might be affected by their progress. The ability to forecast ahead for a group of interacting or related projects is possibly one of the greatest advantages that comes from using earned value methods, yet it is an argument that is rarely put forward.

Whether the DoD really believed that by introducing earned value methods it would get its projects delivered any quicker or cheaper than before is not known by this author, although it must have been a hope. Most experienced managers know that the majority of problems on advanced projects are technical in origin – if a project hits a serious technical problem in a vital area, often little can be done except continue working on it at whatever cost until the problem is cured or the requirement is reduced. The DoD's experience with projects run under earned value conditions has proved this point as it has been observed that once a project starts to slip, that initial rate of slippage is never reduced and frequently gets worse.

Since those early days, project management software tools have developed considerably and the kind of integrated systems that were not around through the 1970s and the early 1980s are now here in abundance. Software specifically designed for both planning, costing and earned value reporting is available but its arrival throws into focus another problem.

In terms of both cost reporting and project planning, an uncoordinated approach was commonly used as 1) it was simpler to operate, and 2) integrated software to make use of coordination was not available. Because of this, cost and schedule reporting could operate in a somewhat undisciplined way that made life easier for both the planners and the accountants; any difficulties that arose could be resolved by discussion and agreement. The advent of integrated software means that a more disciplined approach must be adopted as the elements of discretion and adaptation are absent with mechanized systems.

The simplest and most direct method of updating the project plan is from the data that is captured by the time-bookings and purchasing systems as they usually supply the most accurate and up-to-date information about where time and money are being spent but, as has been said, it is often coded according to the WBS rather than the plan. Some contemporary software will allow WBS codes to be attached to activities in the project network but they can only be used as a method of summarizing costs associated with related groups of activities; they cannot be used as a means of directly updating any activity because several activities can all have the same WBS code and the software has no way of distinguishing between them.

Earned value methods demand a coordinated approach to both cost and schedule reporting; using an integrated software package (that is, one that contains both planning and earned value features) demands that an unambiguous way is found for linking the elements in the WBS with each task in the plan. Both the WBS and the project plan represent two sets of structured knowledge but any system that forges a link between two sets of data demands a discipline of its own that must be recognized and understood. If that discipline is built in at the outset, then the process of control will be much easier; try to put it in when the project is underway and things may become awkward. By creating a WBS that allows the plan to be coded directly from it, a way can be found to structure both the network and the WBS so that they are precisely related and mutually compatible. The most convenient way of doing this is to use the WBS coding as the key code for activity numbering in the network. This fundamental decision will affect the whole project's data structure and has to be taken at the start. Furthermore, it imposes a discipline of thought upon the project planners that they may not have been used to previously.

For complete cost control, any WBS must satisfy the criteria that the work packages are both mutually exclusive and collectively exhaustive; that is to say no work should appear twice and all work must be covered. This principle must not be violated and it must apply equally to the plan. In this respect a matrix type of WBS is particularly useful as it lends itself to generating all the required packages and can also be used to draw the top-level network directly from the matrix. Figure 6.3 shows part of a WBS based on a matrix that was used successfully for managing a development project. As such it should be considered as an example rather than a prescriptive approach as no two projects are alike and the conditions on one may not translate conveniently to another.

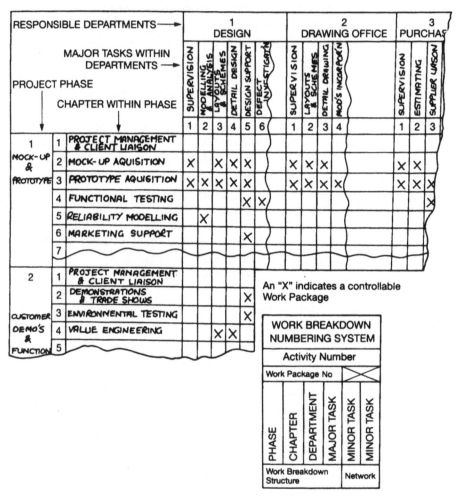

Figure 6.3   Functional work breakdown structure based on a matrix

The most significant feature of Figure 6.3 is that the WBS is expanded by including the principal tasks that the staff normally perform as well as the main subdivisions of the project and the responsible sections of the organization. This feature takes the WBS one step further towards the project plan than is normally the case. The principal tasks that any department of a company can perform are termed major tasks and they are the lowest level in the WBS. A major task is thus the point at which the project plan and the WBS meet. To define the major tasks, a careful look will be needed at what each department actually does as discrete, identifiable and controllable functions. The arrangement of these major tasks, on the basis of the order in which they are performed, will be the starting-point for the project plan.

In Figure 6.3, a formatted sheet has been used to create the WBS. Along the top the major responsible departments have been defined: Design, Drawing Office, Purchasing, etc. Within that definition, the main functions they perform have been specified; for example, for the Design department the main functions are:

1 supervising
2 modelling
3 scheming
4 designing
5 support to manufacture and test
6 specification definition
7 defect investigation
8 meetings and liaison.

When this approach has been put into practice, six, seven or eight main functions have been found perfectly sufficient to define the tasks that a department performs to a level at which adequate plans can be created.

At the left-hand side of the sheet, the main elements of the work to be undertaken can be inserted; these are subdivided into two: Phase and Chapter; alternatively, the main work elements can be subdivided according to the product structure if cost reporting is required in that format. Inserting a cross in a box in the matrix will indicate the identification of a package of work that must be performed and one worthy of control in its own right. This arrangement produces a task-based WBS as the tasks that each department is expected to perform are at its lowest level. A Work Package Number can be derived directly from the position of the cross in the matrix. In this example it is a four-digit number made up from the elements:

- **1st Digit** The Project Phase – a major subdivision of work within the project as a whole (for example, Phase 1: prototype design and construction, Phase 2: Customer demonstrations and full-scale development, and so on)

- **2nd Digit** The Chapter – a major sub-division of work within a project phase (for example Chapter 3, construction of a prototype in Phase 1).

- **3rd Digit** The Responsible Department Code – the area of the company in which the particular skill is to be found (for example, Responsible Department 2 is the Drawing Office). Work Area Code 9 is reserved for bought-out materials and other items of expenditure that do not consume labour but incur costs.

- **4th Digit** The Major Task Code – the particular activity that is required to be done (e.g. Major Task 5 in work area 1 is Design support to manufacture and test). Major tasks 9 and 0 are left free in all cases and can be used to specify any special tasks that are not easily defined by the pre-designated numbers. There is also a work area code 0 which has free fields that can be used to specify any other miscellaneous activities that do not easily fall into any of the other categories.

With this arrangement, a maximum of ten subdivisions can be made within the chapter, phase, department or major task. If more are required either the number of digits must be increased or a letter can be substituted, which will allow up to 26 subdivisions.

Once the WBS has been established, all the work packages in the project will have been identified. The project planning engineer, in conjunction with the project manager, must use judgement in selecting an item to be the subject of a work package in its own right. For example, a major task in the design area may be 'meetings and liaison'; in a large project with regular liaison meetings with the sponsor or other contractors, this may be a significant item of both time and cost and worthy of special control. In a smaller project, even though there will be meetings, these may be considered as part of the normal design process and not singled out. The greater the number of identified work packages, the greater will be the detail contained in the plan and the subsequent reporting, but this must be set against the extra complexity and the need to ensure that times and costs are correctly booked to a multiplicity of task codes.

A basic network should be constructed using the work packages or major tasks to lay out the main logic and establish overall time-scales. The major tasks themselves will be too large and general for both precise logic definition and project control, hence they must be broken down into minor tasks or activities. These activities will specify a definable amount of work to the same level as would be expected in a normal network but they must all emanate from and be contained within their own work package; activities which cross work package boundaries are not allowed. The activities are numbered by adding an extra digit or digits onto the work package number from which they arise. Some planning engineers may see this approach as robbing them of some of the freedom of thought that they had previously enjoyed, and resistance to using it may be encountered. However, this resistance must be overcome; the point to make is that planners should no longer think of planning for activities alone but planning for the total project control process, which includes the costing and the reporting systems.

The major advantage of this approach is that just one number is used throughout; there is never any need to transpose data from one coding system (the WBS) to another (the network codes) in order to update the network with progress or generate the costs associated with work packages. It means the network can be updated with progress directly from the data generated by the time-booking and accounting systems as the codes in both systems are identical. There is no need to employ 'data capture sheets' which require staff to record their working hours against both the cost code (work package number) and the activity number. In practice, when data capture sheets are used either staff don't bother to fill them in or when they do, half the time they are filled in incorrectly as the precise matching that is needed between the cost codes and the activity numbers is not achieved. The benefits of using a single code number throughout cannot be overstressed; an arrangement that involves independently maintaining two sets of data in parallel whilst keeping a strict relationship between the two but using different codes can be one of the biggest sources of errors, confusion and wasted effort, particularly if the project is large and the plan is subject to frequent changes.

Figure 6.4 shows a sample of the basic logic in precedence form drawn from the matrix of Figure 6.3, while Figure 6.5 shows the basic logic's expansion to form the detailed network. Figure 6.5 gives further information as the activity boxes contain details of the grade of labour to be used along with the estimated hours and the activity duration in days.

In the example in Figure 6.5 a standard system of labour coding has been used; this is recommended when you wish to plan company-wide across a range of projects all calling on the same resources. In Figure 6.5, the labour coding system, made up of two letters and a digit, is one that was actually used on aerospace development projects. The two letters

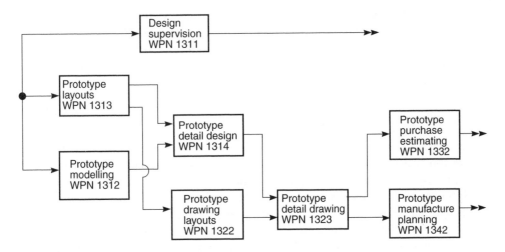

Figure 6.4   Basic task logic is derived from the work breakdown structure

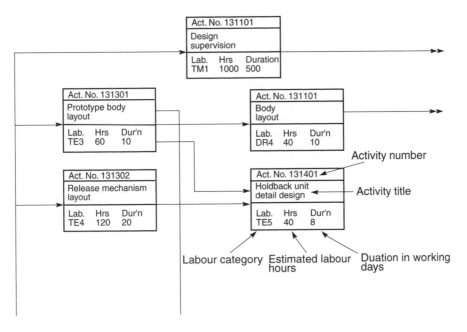

Figure 6.5   Detailed task logic is derived from the basic logic by breaking down the major tasks into minor tasks or activities

indicate the job. The first letter indicates the discipline – T = Technical (Design Engineering), D = Draughting etc.; the second letter indicates the role within that discipline – M = Manager, E = Engineer, etc. The digit at the end indicates the hourly charge rate for costing purposes. Eight standard rates were used into which all chargeable staff were allocated, rate 1 being the highest hourly rate and rate 8 being the lowest.

Thus activity No. 131101 (Design Supervision of the Prototype) requires 1000 hours of technical management (TM) time over a 500-day period at charge rate 1. With the project plan expressed in this form, it can be loaded into a project management software system.

The arrangement described above was used successfully; the use of a single coding system for both the WBS and the network plan resulted in remarkably trouble-free operation when compared to the problems that have been encountered when two different coding systems have been in use simultaneously. Figure 2.1 in Chapter 2 is taken from a project run under this arrangement.

SYSTEMS INVOLVING MULTIPLE CODES

Despite the clear advantages of using a single code as the basis of both the work breakdown structure and the planning there are occasions where using two codes cannot be avoided. This can happen where a company providing products or services to a larger project has a WBS imposed on it by its customer who demands reporting on cost and progress in a prescribed format. From the point of view of a prime contractor or a customer organization, using a common WBS and reporting format across all supplying contractors makes good sense, particularly when it comes to integrating data from a variety of sources, but it can create fundamental problems for the supplying contractors. The customer organization may demand a product-based WBS for valid reasons of its own, ignoring the practical advantages of a task-based WBS at the supplier level; however, a more problematic issue could be the number format.

A customer could devise a work breakdown coding that is eight characters long including both letters and numbers, but what happens if the cost-collection and time-recording system in the supplier company can only accommodate six characters? Clearly an issue like this could go to the heart of the company's accounting system and could be fundamental to the design of all its standard paperwork (for example, time-sheets, invoices, purchase requisitions, and so on) and its data input formats; it could be very difficult to change. The answer lies in the appropriate choice of project management software. Many packages allow multiple work breakdown structures and here one WBS can be used for cost and time collection and thus can be made compatible with the existing company systems while another can be used for reporting to the customer. In this case the WBS code for reporting to the customer acts only as a sort-code which allows data to be reorganized in the required way but plays no part in the data-gathering process. In this case many activities can carry the same customer WBS code if that is required. Furthermore, should there be some errors in the allocation of customer WBS codes to activities, they will not fundamentally affect the operation of the reporting system even if they do produce some small errors in the reported position. The system is summarized in Figure 6.6.

Organizational aspects

Figure 6.7 shows an example of the data structure and organizational relationships plus the principal data flows necessary for an earned value performance measurement system to work. In this case the WBS forms the bridge between the organization structure that defines who is responsible for each task and the network which holds the plan of what is to be done and when. A suitable project management software package or suite of packages is essential to perform all the necessary calculations. Besides the normal start and finish dates, criticalities, etc., it will generate:

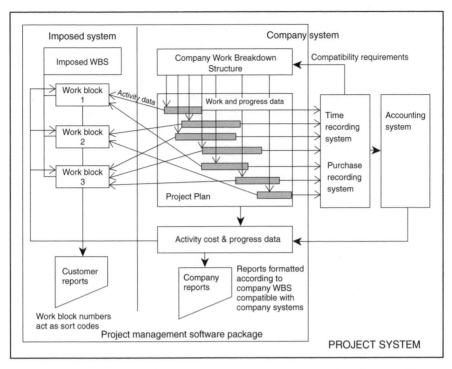

Figure 6.6   Satisfying both customer and company requirements may need a software package that can handle multiple WBS codes, one serving the company systems requiremens while sorting processed data to suit the customer

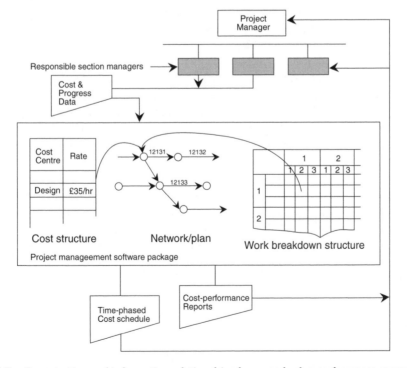

Figure 6.7   Organization and information relationships for earned value performance measurement

- the costed schedules of work which form both the budgets and the instructions regarding what each section manager is expected to perform, and
- the performance reports.

The budgets must be agreed with each section manager before the system is put into operation as no manager is going to be held responsible for budgets to which he has not agreed. Budgets and targets can be set but they have no meaning unless those with authority take responsibility for achievement. Section managers who are sufficiently close to the task and have enough authority must be appointed to take responsibility for performance against their budgets. It is these managers who will receive the cost performance reports and will be expected to take action according to whatever is indicated.

COST BREAKDOWN

In addition to the WBS and the OBS another term, the '**Cost Breakdown Structure**' (CBS), has come into use but this was not a feature of the original DoD specification and the term is not officially recognized in the USA. The CBS has been defined as 'a system for subdividing a project into a) hardware elements and sub-elements, b) functions and sub-functions and c) cost categories to provide more effective management and control of the project'.[1] This is a somewhat ambiguous definition as these divisions might seem either mutually exclusive or overlapping and it leaves it open to the individual as to what this structure is and how it may be used; consequently there are a number of possible interpretations. One obvious and useful interpretation is to attach the values of all the cost accounts to their respective WBS elements and this will result in a costed work breakdown structure. Whether or not this can be deemed to be a cost breakdown structure in its own right is open to debate but it does fulfil the requirement of part a) of the above definition and it does have the merit of being directly related to another fundamental data structure. Another possibility is to take all the work packages and subdivide them according to cost categories such as material, labour and overheads, then recombine all the individual costs into the overall cost categories so that one can see total labour, total materials, etc. Whether this can be deemed to be a *cost* breakdown structure is equally open to debate as it is not a structure in its own right but something that results from other data sets; what importance is attached to such information and what use is made of it rather depends on the project. However, in the context of integrated project planning and control, a more relevant structure might be the cost structure of the organization that is performing the project.

Computerized systems that are capable of planning projects can include resource requirements. When these are allied to the appropriate charge rates, it is possible to put costs on all the activities in the project. A fully costed project is fundamental to earned value performance measurement and the application of the process relies on a computerized system. Thus, from an operational standpoint, the most appropriate cost breakdown structure is that associated with the charge-rates and overheads of the organization performing the project. It is this interpretation that is shown in Figure 6.7.

Notes

1.   Flemming, Q. W. (1988) *Cost/Schedule Control Systems Criteria – The Management Guide to C/SCSC*, Chicago: Probus Publishing Co., p. 506.

7 *Managing With Earned Value Data*

The use of earned value measurement techniques can produce data that gives a valuable insight into the workings of the project, but will be of little value unless project managers act upon the information in a way that preserves the project's objectives. However, what earned value can reveal may also be highly sensitive if it shows a worsening situation, and here the project manager needs to use a degee of discretion

Measuring project progress

In Chapter 5, Figure 5.1 shows the principal elements in the project cycle and it will be realized that using earned value methods has a significant effect on the approach to planning. EV's other major impact is the contribution it makes to the control process. Once the earned value performance measurement system is in operation, each responsible section manager will be required to participate in the control process through: 1) the work that they authorize, 2) their assessment of the amount of progress, and 3) the controlling actions they take. Generating an accurate value for the earned value or BCWP has often been considered as one of the more contentious parts of the whole earned value management process. The generally accepted criterion is that earned value reporting should be both objective and verifiable but sometimes a subjective or an arbitrary element in this must be accepted. However, as the project progresses more activities are completed; the BCWP for a completed activity becomes the Original Budget (OB) and doubt about its value is removed. The greater the numbers of activities that are completed, the less the potential error within the overall project BCWP, as that figure contains a continuously reducing proportion of activities in progress; in effect, progress with the project tends to reduce the errors in the estimate of the overall BCWP. A number of methods for estimating the BCWP are possible; each has its drawbacks, but all are worthy of consideration for different circumstances. The methods can be broadly divided into four categories: subjective assessments, objective measured assessments, rules of thumb and indirect assessment.

SUBJECTIVE ASSESSMENTS

These methods rely on the experienced judgement of individuals close to the work. Examples of this approach are:

a) At intervals that relate to the reporting calendar, either weekly, fortnightly or once a month, the section heads are asked to estimate the percentage completion of each of the activities, for which they are responsible, that are currently in progress.

b) At intervals that relate to the reporting calendar, the responsible section heads are asked to estimate the amount of time they expect to elapse before each of their current activities is complete; that is, they are asked to predict the remaining duration.

Providing a degree of objective honesty is applied, both these methods can work well and are suitable for activities that span perhaps three to five reporting intervals. They tend to be used where there is no *directly* measurable unit of output, but there are clear indicators of progress. For example, the output of test reports from a test programme gives a measure of progress but some aspects of the test programme may be time dependent and the test reports may be clustered towards the end.

 With method a), the BCWP at the reporting point for any activity is given by the formula:

$$BCWP = OB \times \% \text{ complete}$$

where OB is the original budget for the activity

The sum of the BCWP values for all open and completed activities is the overall BCWP for the project at the reporting date. This method was used in the example given in Chapter 3 (see p. 27).

 With method b), using the predicted remaining duration, one needs to assume a uniform rate of spend in each activity. This may not be a valid assumption in all cases but it is reasonably accurate if the activities are small enough. The BCWP at the reporting point for any activity is given by the formula:

$$BCWP = \frac{OD \times BCWS}{ATE + \text{predicted remaining duration}}$$

where OD = Original duration
       ATE = Actual time elapsed

The predicted duration is found by adding the expected remaining duration to the time elapsed since the activity first started; the BCWS is found from the current cost schedule as generated by the computer or by a simple calculation based on a uniform spend rate. Should the original duration be exceeded, the actual time elapsed is substituted for the OD in the above formula to become:

$$BCWP = \frac{ATE \times BCWS}{ATE + \text{predicted remaining duration}}$$

If one was to ask the section heads to provide both figures (and there could be good reasons for doing so), you can arrive at two different estimates of the BCWP. For example, a task is set to last seven weeks with a budget of £7000; if at week 4 the section head estimates the task to be 60 per cent complete and will require another four weeks to complete, what is the BCWP?

By method a) the BCWP is £7000 × 0.60 = £4200

By method b) the BCWP is $\dfrac{7 \times 4000}{4+4}$ = £3500

It is up to the individual which of these figures is more believable and there is nothing to say that the supervisor is wrong in his assessment of the situation; method *b* implies a uniform rate of spend and that may not be the case. Providing that the responsible managers can be trusted to make a reasoned assessment, method a can work well. It might seem easy to hoodwink the system, especially in the early stages of each activity, but as time passes and the assessed progress is not, in fact, being made, it soon begins to show and the manager cannot disguise it.

OBSERVED MEASURED ASSESSMENTS

These methods rely on some form of scoring based on achieving defined milestones or delivering set quantities. Examples include:

c) At each reporting point, an amount of earned value is credited to each current activity according to an agreed method of scoring based on a milestone or an achievement target.

d) At each reporting point, an amount of earned value is credited to each current activity according to the number of work units completed or delivered.

Method c is useful where there is some easily measurable unit that indicates progress or where there are clearly visible milestones that will show progress when they are achieved. For example, in the drawing office, there is a package of work that covers the output of a set of drawings for a certain item. Inspection of the scope of work and discussions with the designer have resulted in the section leader in the drawing office making an estimate of 80 drawings in the final set and a budget of £100 000 for the work. Because of the way the drawings are created, some drawings may be started but not completed until later drawings are done, when some minor details can be finalized. Drawings may not be issued until checked, which may need to be done in batches of related drawings; this can make the rate of issue of drawings somewhat 'back end heavy' as it may be well after the mid-point of the planned duration before the first completed drawings emerge, even though more than half the work may be done. In a case like this, the idea of a uniform rate of output indicating the rate of progress just cannot be applied; here the rule for assessing the BCWP might be: credit 10% (£10 000) of budgeted cost when the activity starts, give another 50% (£50 000) when 25% (20) drawings have been issued, give another 25% (£25 000) when 75% (60) drawings have been issued and give the final 15% (£15 000) when all the work is complete. This pattern reflects the way that output does not indicate work done until nearly the end of the task; with the formula given above, 60% of the task value will be earned when 25% of the required items have been delivered. An arrangement like this is likely to give an accurate assessment of the earned value at the various stages, but there is a drawback. There may be no general rule that can be applied – each case must be treated individually and a unique formula devised. Furthermore, that formula then needs to be incorporated into the earned value process and correctly applied as the project progresses. Software projects have attracted special attention; metrics involving the number of completed source lines of code (SLOC's) have been used as well as a reverse measurement based on the reported numbers of defects per 1000 SLOC's (this value falls in line with a commonly observed pattern as the task approaches completion). The various output achievement targets can be considered as 'milestones' and the same general comments apply to any milestone-based measurement of work accomplished.

The drawing office example shows a situation where work and output are not simply related because of the creative, interactive front-end activities that inhibit initial output, but there are other cases where this is not so, here earned value can be related directly to measured output. Method d can be used and examples could be: 1) any repetitive production process, provided the initial set-up is treated as a separate activity, and 2) construction activities such as laying bricks or pouring concrete. It only requires a suitable cost value to be established for the measured unit of output, for example, £/finished item, £/1000 bricks laid, £/100m^3 of concrete poured, to count the output and compute the earned value. As with method c, a separate unit of value must be computed for each case but there is none of the complication of a special formula.

RULES OF THUMB

These are simple rules for crediting earned value that make no particular pretence to detail accuracy, but, bearing in mind that errors in the combined overall earned value tend to reduce as the project progresses, they are adequate for control. Examples are:

e) Credit 20% of the total activity budget, OB, as the BCWP when the activity is recorded as having started, credit the remaining 80% when it is recorded as complete.

f) Credit 50% of the total activity budget, OB, as the BCWP when the activity is recorded as having started, credit the remaining 50% when it is recorded as complete.

Simple rules such as this are particularly appropriate where activities are of a duration that is typically between one and three reporting periods long and there are many simultaneous activities. The advantage of this approach is that it can be computerized so the earned values can be calculated directly from progress information, regarding activities started and finished, that is entered into the planning system as part of the reporting cycle. If planned activities can be kept relatively short in duration there may be little to be gained by being any more sophisticated.

INDIRECT ASSESSMENT

These methods apply when the earned value is determined by some outside factor. Two cases typically arise: 1) when the activity is time dependent, or 2) when earned value is related to the progress of some other activities. The first case is typical of an ongoing service to the project as a whole, the most obvious example being managing the project: as long as the project continues the management team has to be in place. The second case is typical of a discontinuous service to some particular aspect of the project such as inspection. For example, inspectors are only required when there is something to inspect, usually when there is some aspect of a deliverable system that is 1) nearing completion, 2) being incorporated into something larger, or 3) ready to deliver; when this occurs is entirely dependent on progress with the deliverable system. Methods used in these cases are:

g) Calculate the earned value based on the elapsed time at some predetermined rate of accrual based on a planned level of effort.

h) Calculate the earned value by apportioning an amount from an overall budget based on progress with the controlling activity.

Method g is known as the 'level of effort' approach and is applied to general service activities. If costs are uniformly spread over the activity duration, earned value is credited according to elapsed time; in this case the BCWP is always equal to the BCWS and there is no schedule variance. Actual expenditure may not be uniform and could also be more or less than planned so there can be a cost variance. Levels of effort can be planned to take into account known changes in effort; in that case, expenditure will not be uniform.

Method h is often called the 'apportioned effort' approach. Quite simply, an amount of value from the overall budget is directly credited to the activity based on a fixed relationship with the value earned on a controlling activity to which it is directly related.

It will be clear that there is no single and generally applicable method of assessing the earned value of any activity in a project, particularly if it is a complex project involving a mix of different skills and tasks. Project managers charged with running projects under earned value conditions need to choose the most appropriate methods based on:

- the required degree of accuracy
- the nature of the particular activity
- the practicality and cost of detailed measurement
- the software in use.

It is likely that a mixture of methods will be used in any real project situation.

Dealing with materials and purchases

When earned value was first implemented in the USA, accounting for materials and purchases proved to be a troublesome aspect (the background to this has already been given in Chapter 2). Much of the difficulty stemmed from an unnatural and largely unnecessary requirement to separate materials out and continuously account for them when they are really part of a bulk quantity that could be used on a variety of projects and might only be allocated to a particular project at the point of issue. Putting aside that issue, the diverse nature of purchased items can mean that accounting for them can still be a problem that might need a variety of solutions.

Externally purchased items can be divided into a number of broad categories for which different methods of performance assessment might be applicable. Some suggestions, according to the type of purchase involved, are listed below:

- **Externally purchased services** – This can include anything that is subcontracted out that is not the subject of an earned value reporting arrangement in its own right. Services might be purchased on an item-by-item basis with budget and time-scale for each item, they might be provided on a continuous basis and thus accounted for on a level-of-effort basis, or they might be provided on an as-and-when basis as part of some general contract when an estimated percentage of total value might be appropriate. There is no single approach to assessing the BCWP that can be recommended as each of these is a different case so any of the above methods might be suitable. Actual costs for work performed are usually credited on receipt or payment of the invoices depending on the policy in force.

- **Externally purchased items of equipment and/or tools** – Providing the items are bought specifically for the project, the BCWP values are credited, according to the original price estimates, at the time of delivery or acceptance. ACWP values are credited on receipt of payment of the invoice. However, there may be more than one invoice because there might be a down payment with the order or a series of stage payments, particularly if the equipment is large or expensive. If the stage payment is significant and tied to an observable milestone, the relevant percentage of the total purchase value could be credited to the BCWP at the time of payment.

- **Externally hired facilities** – These are similar to services but could include such things as test houses which are hired rather than purchased. These are normally paid for on the basis of the time they are used; BCWP values can be credited on the basis of the percentage of the planned period of hire. The ACWP can be credited on receipt or payment of the invoices.

- **Externally purchased, project-specific materials** – Single delivery items can be treated in the same way as equipment, this can apply to such things as special forgings, castings or mouldings. With bulk materials such as building sand, that might be delivered over an extended period or supplied on a call-off basis, the BCWP can be credited as a percentage of the total order quantity and the AWCP credited on receipt of the invoices.

- **Externally purchased, non-project-specific materials** – These can be among the most difficult of items to assess. They can include a host of things such as general stock material (sheet, bar, plate, etc.), paints, finishes, sealants, adhesives and fasteners. With construction projects, these items are less common as most materials are specially bought for the project in quantities specified by the quantity surveyor from the architect's drawings. With development engineering projects, this can be more difficult; at the start of the project, there may be no detail design and, at the early stage, the designers might have a wide choice of materials from which they can choose to fabricate the parts. Which materials and processes are chosen only emerge as the design evolves.

  It is difficult to give a firm recommendation for estimating the BCWP as the situations can be diverse; possibly the most useful might be to use an estimated per cent complete figure for the total manufacturing work package as provided by the manufacturing supervisor, or an apportioned effort approach might be applicable if the manufacturing activities have been planned in sufficient detail.

  Other non-project-specific materials might be involved that do not relate to manufactured aspects but to other parts of the project such as the budget for project stationery and office materials, if a separate budget is created for this aspect. In this case BCWP values can be credited on a level-of-effort basis tied to the complete project time-scale.

  ACWP values can be credited on the basis of issues from stores, providing the stores accounting system can recognize the work-package, control account or activity numbers used by the project monitoring and earned value calculation system. This might not be a simple matter as manufacturing may be accounted for in a different way from project staff, particularly if the company does routine production work in parallel with development manufacturing using the same facilities.

Experience in the USA has shown that regardless of the type of earned value management used for material, it is important to try to match the BCWP and ACWP values within the same reporting period. Otherwise, reporting the BCWP in one month and the actual costs in another month could result in misleading cost variances. In order to achieve this match-up of earned value and actual costs, some companies have chosen to use 'estimated actuals' against the earned value.

Performance measurement

The simplest indicators of project cost and schedule performance are the **Cost Variance (CV)** and the **Schedule Variance** (SV). These are elementary measures of the difference between planned and actual spend at a reporting point. They can be recorded at each reporting point and plotted as a time series as the project progresses; an example is shown in Figure 7.1. Cost and schedule variances can be recorded for any work package, control account or the project as a whole; sometimes warning and action limits can be placed on these figures indicating that some action should be taken to contain spending. Variances can be calculated on the values for the individual periods or on cumulative costs from the start of the project; the latter figure is probably more useful.

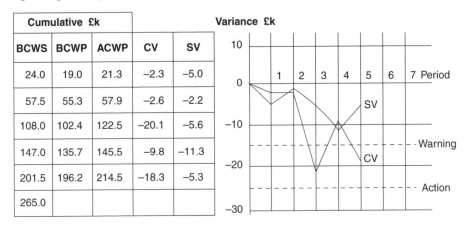

Cumulative £k				
BCWS	BCWP	ACWP	CV	SV
24.0	19.0	21.3	−2.3	−5.0
57.5	55.3	57.9	−2.6	−2.2
108.0	102.4	122.5	−20.1	−5.6
147.0	135.7	145.5	−9.8	−11.3
201.5	196.2	214.5	−18.3	−5.3
265.0				

Figure 7.1   Plotting the Cost and Schedule Variances against time can show a trend, if there is one. Action and warning limits are also shown, the fact that the cost variance passed the warning limit at Period 3 may account for the jump in performance in Period 4, but the more likely explanation is that actual cost bookings have been running ahead of credited earned value in Period 3, possibly because something has been paid for in advance of delivery (for example a down-payment for tooling associated with the manufacture of a major item) which is then corrected in Period 4

The variances can be useful for measuring the absolute cost differences at a reporting point, but they are not the best indicators of overall performance. The two most useful measures of project performance obtainable from the earned value method are the **Cost Performance Index** (CPI) and the **Schedule Performance Index** (SPI). Useful though they are, they say nothing about that other equally, if not more, important aspect of project performance – technical performance; this aspect should never be forgotten when looking at any earned value measurements. CPI and SPI values greater than one indicate performance either in cost or schedule terms that is better than planned, values lower than one indicate a worse position. The CPI is, perhaps, the more useful of the two, it shows the real worth that is being created by the project, thus a CPI value of 0.85 indicates that for every pound spent, only 85 pence worth of value is being created on the basis of the original budget. The behaviour of these two indices can be plotted as the project proceeds; they give a good indication of the real progress and what the future may hold. Figure 7.2 shows a typical situation in terms of the cumulative ACWP, BCWP and BCWS; the indices have been derived and are plotted. Using the indices gives a clearer view of the position than reading the relative ACWP, BCWP and BCWS values. Figure 7.3 shows the pattern of the CPI and SPI under various conditions.

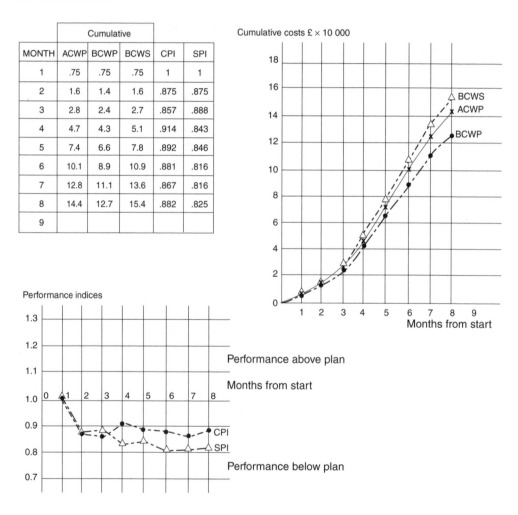

	Cumulative				
MONTH	ACWP	BCWP	BCWS	CPI	SPI
1	.75	.75	.75	1	1
2	1.6	1.4	1.6	.875	.875
3	2.8	2.4	2.7	.857	.888
4	4.7	4.3	5.1	.914	.843
5	7.4	6.6	7.8	.892	.846
6	10.1	8.9	10.9	.881	.816
7	12.8	11.1	13.6	.867	.816
8	14.4	12.7	15.4	.882	.825
9					

Figure 7.2   Relationship between BCWS, BCWP, ACWP and the cost and schedule performance indices. After the fluctuations in the CPI and SPI during the first 4 periods, notice how they settle down to steadier values; this is typical due to the aggregating effect of past data contained within each successive calculation

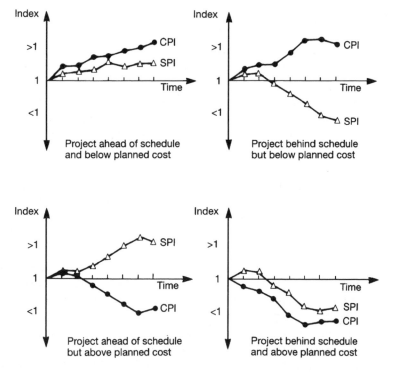

Figure 7.3   Alternative project positions indicated by the movement of the CPI and SPI

An alternative method sometimes advocated for displaying the SPI and CPI performance is the quadrant diagram, as shown in Figure 7.4. Compared to the time based plots shown in Figure 7.3, this is not a good representation of performance as the ability to visualize the trend in the data is completely lost.

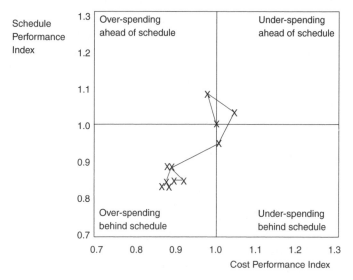

Figure 7.4   Cost and Schedule Performance Indices plotted against each other on a quadrant diagram. This representation is much less easy to interpret than the time series shown in Figure 7.3

The behaviour of the performance indices

Figure 7.5 shows a project in which the original planned BCWS values are given in the top bar against each task number, beneath that is given the actual spread of the BCWP and the ACWP values as they appeared at the time. This project had an initial duration of seven periods but the result was that it actually took ten periods. The cumulative total BCWS, BCWP and ACWP values are given as well as the CPI and SPI values that result at each period's end. The graph at the bottom shows how these values vary. It will be noticed that there are considerable swings in the values of both these indices in the first few reporting periods but as more tasks are completed, and their results are fixed, an aggregating effect occurs and the CPI value settles down to a more accurate and stable level. The behaviour of the SPI has already been discussed in Chapter 3, it too tends to settle but once the original duration (in this example, seven periods) is exceeded it tends towards a value of one, irrespective of the actual schedule performance. The aggregating effect of completed activities means that the further the project progresses towards its conclusion, the more the SPI tends to become a measure of percentage completion rather than a measure of schedule progress. It would have given a better indication of schedule progress for longer if, at some point, the project had been replanned on the basis of an expected longer duration.

If these early swings show high adverse values they can have an alarming effect on staff morale, especially if people are inclined to see them as a direct reflection on their work. Some organizations have thus made it a policy not to openly report CPI and SPI values before three or four reporting periods have passed, or in other cases they have applied an exponential smoothing[1] process to the values in order to damp out variations.

Experience in the USA over the last thirty years of running projects under earned value conditions has revealed some interesting conclusions. In particular, the CPI has consistently shown itself to be a good predictor of overall cost performance. It has been noticed that its value tends to stabilize by about the 20 per cent point in the overall project duration; beyond that its value tends not to vary by more than 10 per cent until the project end. In the majority of cases, variation will be towards a worsening situation rather than an improvement. Part of the explanation for this observation lies in the mathematics of the aggregating effect of the completed activities as demonstrated in the example above. Just as importantly, however, it tends to confirm the well perceived fact that trends in overall performance, once they are established, tend to continue until the end of a project. It might indicate that management's ability to significantly influence matters, once project momentum builds up, is rather more limited than some would wish.

Reporting for earned value measurement

There can be little doubt that obtaining accurate reporting data is one of the most problematic aspects of earned value management and the difficulties often come down to aspects of the internal systems and accounting practices of the firms engaged on the project. By and large, earned value methods were successful in the USA because the companies using EV tended to be large organizations that had regular dealings with the US government, knew the imposed requirements of working on government contracts and were thus prepared to make the investment in appropriate systems, procedures and software. This was not simply a one-way process: the data was also useful for project management and the accounts department.

Task No.	Values £k	1	2	3	4	5	6	7	8	9	10	Totals £k
1	BCWS	20	20	20	10							
1	BCWP	10	10	20	20	10						
1	ACWP	15	15	30	30	15						
2	BCWS		30	30	30	20						
2	BCWP		30	20	20	20	20					
2	ACWP		20	15	20	15	15					
3	BCWS			10	20	20	20					
3	BCWP			5	10	25	20	10				
3	ACWP			15	25	30	25	15				
4	BCWS				10	10	20	20				
4	BCWP					5	15	10	25	5		
4	ACWP					10	15	20	20	10		
5	BCWS				20	30						
5	BCWP					20	20	10				
5	ACWP					15	35	20				
6	BCWS						10	20	10			
6	BCWP						5	10	10	10	5	
6	ACWP						5	5	15	10	5	

	Value in £k									
Total BCWS	20	50	60	90	90	60	30			
Total BCWP	10	40	45	50	80	80	40	35	15	5
Total ACWP	15	35	60	75	85	95	60	35	20	5
Cum. BCWS	20	70	130	220	310	370	400	400	400	400
Cum. BCWP	10	50	95	145	225	305	345	380	395	400
Cum. ACWP	15	50	110	185	270	365	425	460	480	485
CPI	0.667	1.0	0.863	0.784	0.833	0.835	0.812	0.826	0.823	0.824
SPI	0.50	0.714	0.730	0.659	0.725	0.824	0.863	0.950	0.988	1.00

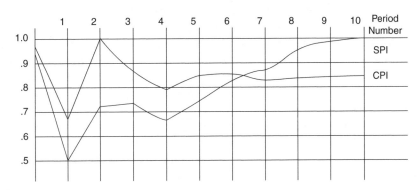

Figure 7.5   The behaviour of the performance indices – these can show initial swings that tend to be damped out by the passage of time and project progress. Note the SPI always has a value of 1.0 at the project's end irrespective of actual schedule peformance

Organizations that undertake significant government contracts tend to have good time recording, purchase accounting, bookkeeping and costing systems in place as part of their normal operating procedures, because the organizations are largely static and have a mostly permanent staff base. This situation is not so true of organizations that are more transient in nature which come together only for the purpose of the project and make use of large numbers of contractors on a more casual basis, possibly on sites remote from the main premises. This can be typical of the construction industry where staff working on the project may not be required to fill in time-sheets, progress is assessed using quantity surveying methods and invoicing is based on material purchase accounts and the numbers on the payroll. Whereas it is possible to assess overall progress and establish the overall cost at any time, it may be very difficult to perform any lower level of earned value analysis; it may be impossible to get any detailed correlation between BCWP and ACWP at anything other than the highest level. This should not however imply that such projects are necessarily out of control, in fact very detailed day-to-day control can be exercised through the site supervisors and there are plenty of examples of construction projects that are completed on time and within budget. Part of that success may, however, come from the practice of awarding contracts for work on the basis of fixed prices with milestone payments, bonuses for early completion and using liquidated damages for late delivery. The difference in this approach is that control is not exercised through the reporting and accounting systems (which is what earned value is really about); it is done by other means, which need be no less effective.

Reporting systems must be set up to gather the cost and progress data. The time-booking system will usually prove convenient for gathering labour cost data and the purchasing or accounts departments will have data on orders, purchases and payments. The relationship to the master plan must be quite clear and the WBS matrix and activity numbering system will help. A dedicated software system with the earned value performance measurement features must be acquired and project management staff must become familiar with its use and accept the disciplines it brings with it; some changes to company procedures may be necessary. Work must proceed through a system of task authorizations; unauthorized work must not be allowed to start. Here the project management software can help as the better-quality packages allow the generation of customized reports and this feature can be used to create authorizations at the appropriate time directly from the plan.

The generation of regular performance reports is vital: responsible managers must see how they are doing at regular and well-defined points. It must be made clear that progress assessments will be required for each work package and responsible managers must submit their reports on time. Resistance may be encountered here but knowing that senior management will be interested in the results can be a great incentive. Project management staff responsible for operating the system must set up a regular routine for themselves and must ensure that authorizations go out on time and that managers know when progress assessments are needed.

Subcontractors can be one of the bigger problems when it comes to timely reporting. This can be made more difficult if there are imposed reporting deadlines set by the sponsor who also demands the most up-to-date information and there is a chain involving a prime contractor and subcontractors. The problem that can arise is that many organizations operate on a monthly accounting cycle, that is, data is gathered during the month then processed at the month's end to produce a complete set of project accounts a week or a fortnight later. This data might then have to be fed into the project management software that will produce the earned value reports – and a few more days will go by. It could be three weeks after the month's end before the earned value reports are available; some of the data contained in it could thus relate to activities undertaken anything up to seven weeks earlier, clearly too late to be of use in direct control. Subcontractor performance data also needs to be collected and incorporated in the reports, so even more time is required as they may have to go through a similar process; by the time the sponsor sees the reports, more than a month has elapsed.

Some organizations, particularly those in the USA connected with advanced technology aerospace development projects, have recently adopted a weekly earned value reporting cycle. It should be remembered that these are also companies which have made large investments in their reporting and accounting software systems and are in a position to impose the required disciplines on the project staff. They are claiming considerable success in maintaining project schedules by this approach; whether this is really due to the effect of earned value measurements or simply that senior management are taking a more detailed interest and becoming more actively involved in solving pending problems one cannot say. There may also be something of an incentive for the project team members through knowing their performance is being actively monitored. There are certainly advantages in adopting tight managerial control particularly when deadlines are important, providing it is not seen as interference or 'micro-management'; how much of this should come through frequent earned value measuement will depend on the required investment in reporting systems and the ease with which the necessary disciplines can be imposed. A balance needs to be struck to ensure that reponsible staff don't get deflected into spending large amounts of time tending to the information system rather than directing the task in hand.

Things can get more complex if subcontractors work on different accounting cycles or admit to publishing their accounts one month in arrears. There is no simple solution to this situation if it arises and it has been a subject of ongoing debate among earned value practitioners; one solution that has been advocated is to use 'flash' data, that is, information supplied as the most up-to-date estimate of progress and actual cost at the reporting point. This is sent to the prime contractor for incorporation to meet the reporting deadline. When accurate data becomes available, some time later, this is substituted for the flash data in the performance measurement system. It must be said that this is not an ideal situation as it leads to doubling the amount of work and is also prone to introducing errors. The answer ultimately lies in all parties agreeing a realistic reporting cycle time and then deciding on just how much more worth can really be attached to having data available at an earlier time. The answer may well be that there is not very much. As has been implied, earned value methods are not the most appropriate for day-to-day control: direct contact with the work, progress meetings and action lists are more effective. Cost and schedule variances may jump from month to month but the overall performance indices will tend to become more stable as the project nears its end, so up-to-the-minute earned value reporting tends to progressively reduce in value as a control mechanism, although not from a measurement viewpoint, in the later stages.

Another problem sometimes encountered is that of the reporting units. It was very clear from the start of earned value assessment in the USA that all reports would be in cost terms: dollars in the first case and no allowance was made for any other unit. Cost is a common denominator when it comes to measuring the worth of the various components of the project, such as labour, services, materials and purchases. Some organizations, because they have found difficulty in obtaining accurate or timely information from their accounting systems, have chosen to use a different unit of measurement, typically the man-week or man-hour. Whereas it is mathematically possible, given a suitable time-booking system, to establish BCWS, BCWP and ACWP values in terms of man-weeks of effort and do the appropriate calculations, this can only be applied to the direct labour element of the project. Few projects consist of nothing but labour; in some projects it may be only a third of the cost. The problem comes in combining values determined in man-weeks with values for purchased items which can only be given as costs. The answer is clear: if an organization wishes to use earned value methods for complete project control then it needs to make the appropriate investment in its data gathering and accounting systems so that all data can be reduced to costs.

Earned value reports

What reports are produced and the formats used can vary according to the requirements of the various parties involved in the project. When earned value methods were first applied, the whole process was embedded in a very prescriptive series of US DoD procedures. These included a number of precisely defined report formats of which the most significant were the Cost Performance Report (CPR) and the Cost/Schedule Status Report (C/SSR). The CPR was designed for complex, high-cost contracts and was defined by five formats: 1) earned value data by WBS element, 2) earned value data by functional category (design, manufacturing, test, facilities hire, etc.), 3) changes to the baseline, 4) actual and projected staffing levels, and 5) variance analysis explanations. The C/SSR is a simpler version of the CPR, used for less complex, less costly contracts below the CPR threshold and only contains two formats – earned value data by WBS element and variance analysis explanations. With the C/SSR, the planned value and earned value can be assessed at any level deemed logical by the project manager whereas the CPR demanded a more rigorous assessment at the control account and work package level. The principal data contained in the C/SSR are:

- **At project level**
    1. Contractor and contract details
    2. Programme details
    3. Report period number
    4. Original target cost
    5. Negotiated contract changes
    6. Current target cost (4 + 5)
    7. Estimated cost of authorized, unpriced work
    8. Current budget base (6 + 7)
- **At activity level**
    9. Activity number
    10. Cumulative BCWS
    11. Cumulative BCWP
    12. Cumulative ACWP
    13. Current schedule variance (Culmulative BCWP – BCWS)
    14. Current cost variance (Cumulative BCWP – ACWP)
    15. Budgeted cost at completion
    16. Estimate at completion
    17. Variance (16 –15)

- **Overall**
   18 General and administrative costs in categories 9 to 17
   19 Overall work package totals in categories 9 to 17.

This produces a suitably comprehensive report on the earned value position of any work package or activity. Standard report formats were also specified and these have been followed by the specialist earned value software packages. An example of a CPR document generated by the *Cobra* package is shown in Figure 8.3 in Chapter 8. It contains an additional split of data between the current period and the cumulative BCWS, BCWP, ACWP and associated variances when compared to the simpler C/SSR; it also shows the general format used for reporting on US government contracts.

   Although the C/SSR format is a very comprehensive one, it requires the specialist earned value performance measurement software to produce it for anything other than the simplest projects. In many cases this will not be necessary, particularly if one is not committed to the full rigours of a US government approach. Simpler reporting formats are used that are generally restricted to variance reports and performance reports.

VARIANCE REPORT

- **At project level**
   1 Programme details
   2 Report period number
   3 Work package (control account) number
- **At activity level**
   4 Activity number
   5 Cumulative BCWS
   6 Cumulative BCWP
   7 Cumulative ACWP
   8 Current schedule variance
   9 Current cost variance
   10 Budgeted cost at completion
   11 Latest revised estimate
- **Overall**
   12 Overall work package totals in categories 4 to 11.

PERFORMANCE REPORT

- **At project level**
   1 Programme details
   2 Report period number
   3 Work package (control account) number
- **At activity level**
   4 Activity number
   5 Cumulative BCWS
   6 Cumulative BCWP
   7 Cumulative ACWP
   8 Current schedule variance

9 Current cost variance
10 Schedule performance index
11 Cost performance index
- **Overall**
  12 Overall work package totals in categories 4 to 11.

An example of a typical variance report is shown in Figure 8.5 in Chapter 8 (p. 107) and a typical performance report is shown in Figure 2.1 in Chapter 2 (p. 16). Both these reports were generated using the earned value features of standard project management planning packages. They do not conform to the requirements of a CPR or C/SSR but they are adequate for normal management control purposes.

Graphical representations of the performance indices and the variances can be helpful in visualizing how the project has been performing since its start. Examples of plots of variances and indices have been given in Figures 7.1, 7.2, 7.3 and 7.5. Brave project managers may even choose to plot variations in the EAC and the estimated completion date. Figure 7.6 shows how this can be done.

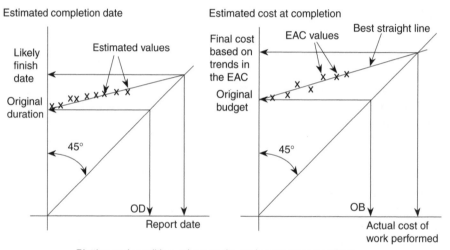

Plotting end condition values as the project progresses allows
a final estimate to be made based on the trends in these values

Figure 7.6 Slip diagram techniques can be used to forecast the end conditions for both time and cost by tracking variations in the EAC and the estimated completion date at each reporting point. Projecting forwards can give an estimate of the final position well in advance of a formalized assessment

Project managers using diagrams such as those shown in Figure 7.6 would be well advised not make the results generally available or well known. If slippage in the programme comes to be seen as the accepted way that things are progressing, it could demotivate the team and turn an estimate into a prophecy that fulfills itself because everyone expects it.

Interpreting the project position

Despite the detailed costs, mathematics and forecasts, it should always be remembered that earned value calculations only provide a very limited view of a project – they have nothing to say about what is actually going on within the project. When it comes to understanding what these reports mean, you must look into the workings of the project; earned value might indicate there are slippages and overruns but gives no clue as to the cause or what might be done about it. All the normal project progress information must still be retained within the overall project control system, including written explanations of deviations from plan, forecasts of future situations and problems outstanding that need to be resolved. An example of a status report is given in Figure 7.7. It shows some earned value data but it gives a great deal more information about what is actually happening in the work package during the reporting period; this may be more valuable to the project manager than pure numerical data. One should always remember that earned value reports are an addition to the normal progress reports, not a substitute for them.

Perhaps two of the most significant questions are who should see the earned value reports and how should they be viewed? This is not an idle question as information contained within them, particularly if it shows predictions of a cost or a schedule overrun, could be seen as potentially explosive. There is no question that some senior managers, either through zeal, ignorance, pressure upon them or a belief about how people should be managed, have a great deal of difficulty in coping with estimates that show a project slip or a cost overrun, particularly if they are in a fixed price or a liquidated damages contract situation for which they may be ultimately responsible. Putting undue pressure on the staff to improve performance or using threats can be counter-productive, it can simply lead to people attempting to cover up or misreport the situation to appear more favourable. Alternatively, it could result in people reverting to indifferent or uncommitted behaviour as they reason that the senior management really do not understand the situation or have no creative solutions to the problem, so why should anyone pay anything other than lip-service to them? Slippages and overruns can come about due to a variety of reasons and they do not necessarily have to be anyone's fault. For example: 1) some external aspect of the project's circumstances could change, over which the project might have no control, 2) an unexpected failure could occur on a test that requires a lengthy investigation programme that might even lead to major redesign, or 3) a supplying contractor could suddenly run into difficulties. Each of these is a potential cause of a delay and an overrun; in fact, I experienced all of these during my project management work – none could have been envisaged at the planning stage.

All forecasts and estimates, if they are made through reasoned assessment, should be taken seriously as they can contain valuable information about a developing situation that should be an aid to planning the way forward. It must always be recognized, however, that all forecast information is potentially sensitive if it shows any variance from the plan; where slippages are indicated they could become a self-fulfilling prophecy if the forecasts come to be common knowledge, particularly if they appear 'official'. The other important point is that forecasts made using the earned value formulae are essentially straight-line projections based on the performance ratios to date. They contain no information about developing future situations and make no allowance for the unforeseen occurring at any point in the future. For this reason, earned value data and the associated forecasts should be distributed only to those with a genuine need to know and they should always be accompanied by a reasoned explanation of the project situation, including those many aspects that are simply not addressed by purely numerical information.

AW	PROJECT STATUS REPORT		

Project Ref. No PA – 03	Project title POWER UNIT DEVELOPMENT	Issue 9	Date 16/6/92
Work Package No 2614	Work Package Title LIFE CYCLE TESTING	Section Head J ROBBINS	

Original Baseline Budget	£ 20,500	Current Baseline Budget	£ 25,350
Original Completion Date	4/9/92	Current Completion Date	25/9/92

Issue No. 1	Date	1/3/91	Issue No. 4	Date	12/6/92

BCWS (Current Budget) £ 15,650	ACWP (Current Budget) £ 17,394	BCWP (Current Budget) £ 16,050

Estimated Cost at Completion	£ 27,464	Cost Variance at Completion £ 2114 (+) (+/–)	

Variance as a % of Budget	Original Baseline 33·97%+	CPI	This Period 0·923
	Current Baseline 8·34%+		Last Period 0·930

Estimated Date at Completion	23/9/92	Variance 0·4(–) Weeks (+/–)	

Variance as a % of Schedule	Original Baseline 27% +	SPI	This Period 1·026
	Current Baseline 1% –		Last Period 0·985

Summary of Current Position		
Progress SATISFACTORY AT PRESENT	Costs SLIGHT UPWARD TREND SINCE LAST REVISION	Staffing SATISFACTORY

Technical TWO SPEED GOVERNOR FAILURES NOTED. EXCESSIVE VIBRATION AT 200 HRS PROBLEM TRACED TO DRY BEARING, NEW SEALS NEEDED.	Facilities TEST INTERRUPTED BY REQUEST TO 'BORROW' VARIOUS ITEMS.

Problems encountered or foreseen TESTS MAY BE HELD UP WAITING FOR NEW DESIGN OF OIL SEAL. GOVERNOR 'STICKING' STILL BEING INVESTIGATED BUT SHOULD NOT HOLD-UP TEST.
Tasks/Actions to be undertaken in the next period COMPLETION OF LOW TEMPERATURE RUNNING, STRIP & INSPECT, INSTALL NEW OIL SEALS START HIGH TEMPERATURE RUNNING.
Comments by Section Head So far so good, high temperature test may be more severe test than previous.

Compiled by L.K TURNER	Circulate to JKR. PL, RFG & FILE	Signed PROGRESS ENGINEER	Signed SECTION HEAD

Figure 7.7   A project status report for a work package – note the earned value data along with other highly relevant information about the progress that is actually being made

Revisions to the baseline

Earned value performance measurement was founded on the idea that the project could be seen in sufficient detail for an accurate plan to be constructed that would show all the major blocks of work and the proper time phasing until the very end. For certain types of project, for example, routine construction, road building or ship building, this can hold good in the general sense even though there may be minor variations to the plan. Other types of project, particularly those with a high degree of technical innovation, for example, weapons system development and some major software systems projects, can have very different features. These projects are characterized by changes and surprises; the unexpected is the one thing that can be expected and there are frequent revisions to whatever plans have been made. In certain respects, one could say these projects are perhaps the least suitable for earned value methods, yet it was on just such projects that the whole approach was started. It was the desire to place certainty and foresight into projects that were inherently uncertain that was a principal motivator. If all projects were of the routine and highly predictable type, nobody would ever have started down the performance measurement route – it simply would not have been worth it.

When earned value methods began, the US DoD laid great emphasis on the development of a complete and detailed plan for every phase of its projects as early as possible. To think that an initial plan, even after a full review, would remain stable over the duration of the project in the face of inherent uncertainties that must have existed was an unrealistic expectation and recognized as such. The DoD did, however, improve the chances of stability by allowing the plan to contain contingencies that could be used to overcome difficulties and maintain the plan without too many deviations and thus uphold the overall integrity of the baseline. In particular, it allowed the provision of a management reserve within the budget at completion that could be distributed to existing or new activities that were within the overall framework, if circumstances demanded. An approach similar to this can be recommended in any project situation where there is an element of uncertainty.

The development of a baseline plan in which all can have confidence at the start is essential to the effective use of earned value methods. This was recognized in the USA by the adoption in 1994 of the Integrated Baseline Review process in which the plan could be thoroughly scrutinized before it was acccepted as the base position from which all performance would be measured. Integrated Baseline Reviews take place after contract award. A particular aspect of the review process is a thorough assessment of the risk areas in the project plan. It demands that risks are identified and assessed in the areas of 1) technical performance, 2) adequacy of the budget provision, 3) overall time-scale, 4) availability and suitability of resources, and 5) appropriateness of the management process. This is a very comprehensive review designed to ensure that a thorough understanding of all the project issues exists on both sides. The important point to note is the detail of the planning and the thoroughness of the evaluation before the full performance measurement process is implemented. This approach has not tended to be mirrored by British practice, which lays great emphasis on competitive tendering, often with relatively short periods in which to generate the full proposal and submit it. Contracts are then frequently let on a fixed-price basis; there is no proper review and risk assessment but the project proceeds through a series of change orders that are agreed between the sponsor and the contractors to cover developing situations that were not envisaged in the original submission.

In any effective project control system, the handling of changes is a significant element.

No project can be properly managed if uncontrolled changes can creep in; if that happens it can lead to a chaotic situation and a lack of overall direction. However, changes cannot always be avoided; they may be forced upon the project by events and they may be essential if the project is to move forward in a proper manner. There is simply no benefit in trying to direct people to report against an old plan that simply does not reflect what is being done or what is intended, particularly if planned work is no longer needed and new and unplanned tasks must be performed instead. To fail to admit changes in the face of obviously altered circumstances or new knowledge can be as harmful as uncontrolled change. All projects need a proper change control procedure to:

- formally acknowledge change that has come about due to deviations from existing plans or altered circumstances,
- assess proposals for change that arise from new knowledge about the project situation
- ensure that approved changes are properly incorporated in the project plan and acted upon.

As changes are accepted and incorporated, the original baseline plan will be increasingly less relevant as a statement of the way ahead. It can lead to the development of two plans: a baseline for reporting purposes and a working plan for day-to-day control. This is not ideal and the more the two plans deviate the more difficult the whole reporting situation can become. It must therefore be recognized that baseline plans are likely to have a limited operational life and there will come a time when all the changes must be rationalized into a new baseline. This is true of any project containing inherent uncertainty.

Besides changes, baselines for both budgets and time-scales can be subject to other problems, some of which are the result of management actions.

FRONT-END LOADED BASELINES

Front-end loaded baselines can occur when work in the near-term is perceived clearly and can be estimated precisely but longer-term work is less well defined. This lack of definition may exist for perfectly valid reasons as some of the long-term work may be dependent upon the results of the near-term work. There can be a temptation to put in realistic budgets for near-term work while underpricing longer-term work in the expectation that contract changes or budget amendments will be negotiated in the intervening period to cover any overspends that may arise later on. Unscrupulous contractors may also be able to exploit lack of knowledge on the part of the sponsor, particularly in highly specialized areas of technology to cover a low initial contract budget. The effect may not become apparent until well into the project when actual costs suddenly begin to diverge from the baseline plan and there is flood of change requests.

RUBBER BASELINES

This problem was particularly prevalent in the time before there were integrated project planning and costing software packages. In the early days, because these two aspects were separate, it was possible to shift the budgets for work without actually shifting the appropriate activities in time. Although this practice was prohibited under formalized earned value contractual arrangements, some contractors became quite clever at bringing budgets

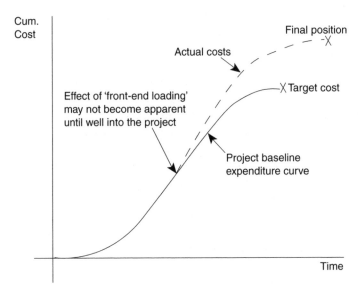

Figure 7.8   The effect of front-end loading can disguise a potential cost overrun during the early part of the project

forward without the corresponding movements in the planned work. The effect was similar to front-end loading by a slow process of subtly altering the baseline at each reporting period, thus disguising the potential for a cost overrun.

BASELINE REVISIONS

The fact that most projects are subject to variations, from whatever cause, was recognized from the time that earned value methods were first devised. It was also recognized that continuing to measure progress against an out-of-date plan would, in the end, lead to a totally

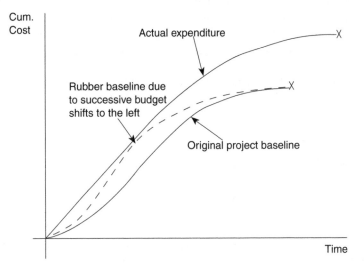

Figure 7.9   The 'rubber baseline' – continuous revisions to the budget timing can also disguise a potential cost overrun

false view. Customer organizations might simply have to swallow hard, sweep up all the changes, for better or worse, and create a new baseline position at a time when it is deemed that the current baseline plan no longer gives a true representation of the intended work.

The DoD's approach to this problem was to allow two conditions: 'reprogramming' and 'replanning'. The essential difference is that reprogramming involves allocating additional funds to the baseline in excess of the contract value and possibly schedule changes that exceeds the contract schedule dates, while replanning allows the contractor to move the activities in time without altering their budgets. A contract change is not required if the work content has not changed. This is a purely US approach but it does have the merit that it stops changes to the plan becoming the subject of a contract change where they don't involve a change in the project budget. However, this condition might not apply if the contractual arrangement involves some form of delivery incentive or liquidated damages; if this is the case, a change in the schedule, irrespective of the budget, would have to be accompanied by a contract change. Whether or not one would choose to use the distinction between 'replanning' and 'reprogramming' is a matter that needs to be agreed between the parties when the control procedure is set up.

Reprogramming always involves a change to the baseline, and four conditions were identified:

1 **Eliminate the schedule variances** – With this method the total budgeted cost for work scheduled (BCWS) is made equal to the budgeted cost for work performed (BCWP) and a new baseline is projected forward from the current BCWP. This will result in a baseline with the same overall time-scale but more compressed activities, this additional priority may result in an increase in the baseline cost at completion which must be accepted in the revised plan. Such an approach could be used where the end date for the project is absolutely fixed, for example, the opening of a new stadium for the 2008 Olympic Games: once the date is announced it cannot be allowed to slip.

2 **Eliminate the cost variances** – Here the BCWP is made equal to the current actual cost of work performed (ACWP) and the new baseline is projected forward from a new budget position based on the current BCWS plus the ACWP less the BCWP at the point of implementation of the new baseline. This creates a baseline above the ACWP line, thus the schedule variance will continue to be negative even though the cost variances disappear.

3 **Eliminate both the schedule and cost variances** – This is a complete reprogramming of the whole project with a new baseline projected forward from the current ACWP, at which point all variances are eliminated.

4 **Preserve all variances** – In some cases, the existing variances are small enough to be tolerable and no adjustment to existing data is made.

Which of these conditions is applied depends on the circumstances and the degree of reprogramming involved. Option 1 might be applicable in some circumstances, particularly if there is known to be some slack in the programme, if activities can be 'crashed' or the end date is absolutely fixed. Option 2 is something of a mathematical trick to ensure that the schedule variances remain negative even though additional funds have been allocated to speed up the completion of the project. In practice this awkward and somewhat artificial method is rarely used; the justification for such an approach would have to be political rather than practical. Option 3 is a chance to inject new realism into the project plan free of any artificial constraints; it must be considered the best option unless there are overriding political considerations to do otherwise. The graphical interpretation of the first three of these options is given in Figure 7.10.

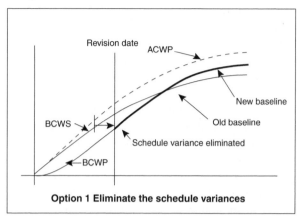

Option 1 Eliminate the schedule variances

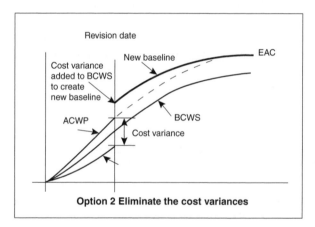

Option 2 Eliminate the cost variances

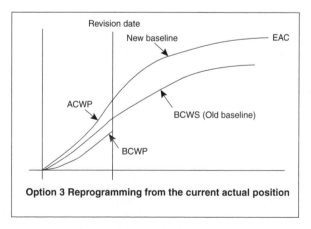

Option 3 Reprogramming from the current actual position

Figure 7.10   Options for revising the project cost baseline to reflect the current situation. Option 3 is probably the most realistic, unles there are good reasons to adopt Option 1; Option 2 is not recommended (source: Flemming, Q. W., *The Management Guide to C/SCSC*)

Once a new baseline plan has been generated, reporting against the original baseline becomes irrelevant and the whole performance measurement process starts from a new position. In the case of Option 3, the CPI and SPI values revert to 1.0. In practice, issuing a new baseline programme is done only when the original plan has become so out-of-line with the current situation that the relationship between the two is no longer meaningful. Nevertheless, plans issued to the project team should always reflect the latest thinking and as soon as any changes from the baseline are introduced, errors in the earned value calculations begin to appear although initially they may be small enough to ignore.

Very often the generation of a new baseline requires considerable clerical and planning effort as it will be normal to assess not only the current position but the entire future plan. Few projects of any magnitude are completed without the creation of revised baselines at some point in their lives; as much as possible this process should be restricted to the few occasions that are really necessary but, when a new baseline is created, the changes should be as comprehensive and far-sighted as possible.

Earned value methods are an aid to the project manager, they are not an end in themselves. The data they produce can be of great use for the insight they can give into the progress that is being made and what the future may hold. However, EV does demand reporting against a fixed plan; sometimes events dictate that the plan is not going to be met and something needs to change. Performance measurement may be very useful, but when rapid changes are needed to keep the project on track they have to be made irrespective of the reporting requirements. The dead hand of the past should never be allowed to rule the future.

Note

1 Exponential smoothing was invented by R. G. Brown in the 1950s as an aid in making short-term forecasts, principally for the next time period ahead of the latest figure. Brown's formula is a form of mathematical smoothing to establish the trend in a series of more erratic data. As well as forecasting, it can be used for reporting purposes; the formula is:

> The latest smoothed value = the previous smoothed value + a proportion of the difference between the latest actual value and the previous smoothed value.

In mathematical terms this is given as:

$$S_T = S_{T-1} + a(V_T - S_{T-1})$$

where

S_T = Smoothed value at time T (that is, at latest time)

S_{T-1} = Smoothed value at time T−1 (that is, smoothed value at the previous period)

V_T = Actual observed value at time T (that is, latest observation)

a = Smoothing constant

This formula is sometimes revised for easier working to give:

$$S_T = (1-a)S_{T-1} + aV_T$$

The weights attached to each observed value in the series of values that make up any smoothed value, S_T, form an exponential series as each decreases by a fixed fraction $(1- a)$ over the previous, with the greatest weight being attached to the most recent observation.

For reporting purposes, values smoothed by the exponential process are used, as data that exhibits considerable variation may be subject to misinterpretation if too much notice is taken of the local fluctuations. The degree of sensitivity in the resulting smoothed values to changes in the most recently observed data is controlled by the factor a. If a is set to 1, the new smoothed value will be equal to the latest observation and there will be no smoothing. If a is set to 0, all variation from the initial position is removed and the smoothed figure remains constant at the initial value. In practice, setting a between 0.1 and 0.2 is found to give the most appropriate smoothed figures both for reporting and forecasting purposes.

8 Software for Earned Value Methods

In many aspects of contemporary project management, software systems have become an essential part of the process and earned value is no different. It could be argued that the advent of high-speed computing in the mid-1950s created project management as we know it today; methods such as critical path analysis would have been quite impractical without it. Unfortunately, however, the theorists ran ahead of the practitioners. Although critical path and PERT methods were fine in theory, in the early days the practice was often made difficult by decidedly less than adequate software. So problematic was it that some project managers actually abandoned drawing and analysing networks during the 1970s and reverted to hand-drawn Gantt charts, task lists and weekly progress meetings. However, the PC revolution that started in the mid-1980s has reversed that position and a host of reliable and affordable project management software is now available that can perform a wide variety of tasks. Unless the project is very small, most project managers have access to some form of planning software.

It has already been said that the original take-up of earned value methods in the USA was slow and that lack of suitable software must have been a contributory factor, particularly after the failure of PERT/Cost, which embodied earned value principles. However, the lack of suitable software was not the only problem as in some cases, the data structure and mode of operation did not support an earned value approach.

A cautionary tale

From the late 1970s to mid-1980s, I was involved in the management of an Anglo-US air-weapon development project; because of its high value, the British prime contractor was obliged to install earned value methods when the USA decided to join the project, after it had been underway for some years. The plan was not contained in any single document as it existed in a variety of forms – networks, supplies schedules and trials lists which bore a relationship to one another – while the work breakdown structure, used for cost collection, had only a loose relationship to the various aspects of the plan. When this was coupled with a project involving nine major subcontractors, all developing different aspects involving thousands of components to be made within a very complex and interlocked plan, the problems become obvious. No possibility existed for automatically assessing the progress of any specific activity and tying it to anything but the broadest work blocks in the cost collection system. In practice, to comply with the US earned value requirement was immensely time-consuming: everything had to be done manually and the result was of dubious accuracy. When the USA pulled out of the project, the first thing the British company did was to abandon earned value measurement – it had all been too troublesome for what little of value was produced.

The reason for dispensing with EV methods did not lie with principles of EV itself; the problem was that when the project started it was an all-British affair for which earned value methods were never considered and appropriate data structures were never created. Costs were collected and allocated to the work blocks in the work breakdown structure so project cost against the WBS budget was always known. Progress, however, was a completely different matter, as the network was used primarily as a way of planning future work from whatever position the project found itself in; there was no reporting against a 'baseline' position for anything but the very highest level. This situation stemmed from another problem: the plan was extremely complex, with many thousands of activities. The customer required it to be planned and costed in great detail so that a position could be fixed from which all changes could be costed and agreed, a baseline position but based primarily on cost; time was a secondary issue. This was the result of yet another problem: by the time the prime contractor had set out a baseline position it could take three to four months to get this agreed among all the contractors, who each had to give their input. When a baseline position was finally agreed, it was already out of date as a working document. Furthermore, the project was plagued with technical difficulties that needed work-around plans to be developed on virtually a daily basis. For this reason the baseline plan was never viewed as something to report against, as it was always out of date; managers looked upon the plan that was created as a continuously updated view of what to do in the future and that became the principal task of the planners. As tasks were completed they simply dropped off the plan and historic schedule information about them was lost. None of this should imply that the project did not make progress or that there was no control. For example, when some serious cost issues faced the project, much of the test work was removed from the plan in order to keep within budget, an indicator that very drastic controlling actions were taken. The project was completed successfully as a purely British project and the weapon went into RAF service. With hindsight one could say that the use or non-use of earned value methods would have had no bearing on the outcome of this project, which was subject to some serious technical problems that required a significant effort in cost and time to overcome. The requirement for the weapon was a national priority; unless the problems had been viewed as intractable or the strategic situation changed, the project was going to continue to its conclusion.

Lack of suitable software undoubtedly contributed to the three to four months it took to create and agree the plan; huge numbers of activities had to be integrated across the nine participants, using comparatively crude network analysis tools which were quite useless for handling the massive and complex supply schedules created to deal with the large amounts of hardware that had to be made, assembled and tested. This initial difficulty led to a position where the concept of reporting against a baseline plan had little real credibility with a project team which regarded plans as a transient view of a changing future, rather than an established view from which all deviations could be measured. This attitude was reinforced by the frequent changes of plan that resulted from the many technical and manufacturing problems which hampered this development project throughout most of its life.

The problems were all made worse by the fact that the project planning packages of the time could not translate the project network into a Gantt chart, as a result, no visual representation of the project plan was possible, nor was any software available that could perform earned value calculations. It is thus not surprising that, under the circumstances, earned value methods proved virtually impossible to implement in a satisfactory way and were dispensed with as soon as the requirement was no longer mandatory.

Contemporary software

The above tale relates to a time about 17 years ago when the tools available today just did not exist – this lack of suitable software undoubtedly contributed to an already difficult situation. Today, many of the problems can be resolved with current tools but certain basic issues still remain. Earned value methods have always relied on the fundamental idea that a project can be seen from start to finish with reasonable clarity at the beginning. If this condition is not met because of too many unknowns or later events in the project are to be determined by the outcome of earlier events, such as in a pure research project, then earned value methods are not the most appropriate. Earned value methods are best suited to projects of the more routine type or those that are well understood at the outset. Remember, earned value concepts started from standard costing applied to stable industrial processes, not unstable projects. If a large amount of experimental and developmental work is expected, then a great deal of initial planning and feasibility study work needs to be done to establish a baseline plan to which all can agree **before the main project starts**. The scale of this task should not be underestimated if the project is complex.

Many of the contemporary project planning and management software packages contain:

- network analysis
- bar chart drawing
- allocation of resources to activities
- allocation of cost rates to resource codes
- work breakdown structuring
- project costing and budgeting
- resource scheduling
- progress reporting
- report generation
- earned value calculations.

Because of the very comprehensive nature of these packages, they can do much more than simply hold the project plan, analyse it for its properties and generate Gantt charts. The ability to add resources and cost means the planning system can now become part of the estimating and budget compilation process, which in earlier times was viewed as a separate process. The ability to generate costed schedules and hold reported progress means the potential for earned value analysis is contained within the basic operational structure, providing a link can be created with the accounting system. This was the essence of the PERT/Cost method of the early 1960s which failed due, among other things, to inadequate software, but whose basic concept is now achievable thirty years later. Earned value calculation is a relatively recent innovation that has only become general during the last ten years. An example of a contemporary project planning system is *Primavera Project Planner* which contains earned value analysis features as part of the package.

Not all packages contain full earned value features that include the comprehensive reporting required by the US DoD, but some vendors offer add-on modules which enhance the basic system. An example is *Artemis Cost View,* a full cost management system which can be run in conjunction with *Artemis Project View. Artemis Project View* is the direct descendent of *Prestige PC* from K&H used in Figure 2.1 (see p. 16); when this project planning software was acquired by Artemis Systems from K&H in the early 1990s the earned value features were removed, but the usefulness of this facility has resulted in earned value analysis being reintroduced in the latest version. *Artemis Cost View* is the direct descendant of another K&H product, *I/CSCS*.

Unlike the integral earned value features in a package like *Primavera Project Planner*, specialist add-on packages can be run in stand-alone mode by importing data from other sources as well as running in conjunction with their sister products. *Cobra* is an example of an add-on or stand-alone package; it is designed to run in conjunction with *Open Plan* although *Open Plan* does have some earned value features. Besides *Open Plan, Cobra* can link directly with *Microsoft Project* and *Primavera Project Planner,* to import schedule data; it can also import data from other planning packages through the creation of transaction files. Because the original customers for this specialist software were mostly contractors to either the US Departments of Defense or Energy, the output report formats are similar and reflect their intended compliance with the US DoD data item specifications for reporting. Those project planning and management packages with integral earned value features do not tend to follow the DoD formats, even though they may do many of the standard earned value calculations, as they are intended for more general application and would not meet the strict budgeting and reporting requirements of the US earned value purists.

Specialist software for cost and schedule control

Taking *Cobra*, as an example, a brief description will enable you to see how the basic principles are applied in a current product. Two basic data sets are required: the work breakdown structure (WBS), which defines the work to be done, and the organization breakdown structure (OBS), which defines the structure of the company or companies that will do it. This structure stems directly from the original DODI 7000.2 requirement and reflects the intended market for this software, as well as illustrating how those original decisions taken over thirty years ago are still influencing current practice. Each element of the WBS must be identified with a single element in the OBS (that is, one unique block of work is the responsibility of one particular department) and the two taken together represent a 'control account' or 'cost account'. Within each cost account, lower-level elements of work can be defined and these are termed 'work packages'. Thus the basic screen which appears at the start and shown in Figure 8.1 is a split view which shows, in the upper half, the cost accounts defined by the combination of the WBS and OBS codes and, in the lower half, the work packages associated with the selected cost account. Once the basic data has been organized into these structures, more detailed information about each work package can be entered.

Cobra provides a complete costing facility, but, before any work can be costed, the items that incur cost have to be established along with their cost rates and appropriate overheads. The split-screen format is used to define, in the upper half, the budget elements – engineers, technicians, etc. – and in the lower half, the calculations that are used to determine the cost figure. Costs can be planned, budgeted and collected at either the cost-account or work-package level, hence planning can be done at a higher level for blocks of work that will be broken into more detail at some later point. However, earned value calculations can only be performed at the work-package level, hence it is this level that reporting must be done if it is wished to use this feature; this, in turn, may have implications for the organization's

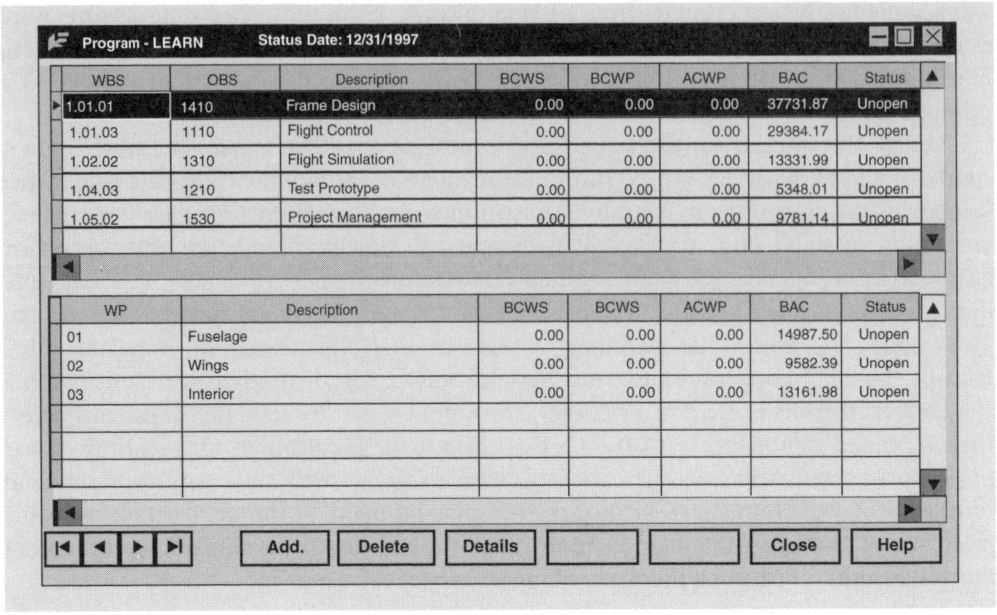

WBS	OBS	Description	BCWS	BCWP	ACWP	BAC	Status
1.01.01	1410	Frame Design	0.00	0.00	0.00	37731.87	Unopen
1.01.03	1110	Flight Control	0.00	0.00	0.00	29384.17	Unopen
1.02.02	1310	Flight Simulation	0.00	0.00	0.00	13331.99	Unopen
1.04.03	1210	Test Prototype	0.00	0.00	0.00	5348.01	Unopen
1.05.02	1530	Project Management	0.00	0.00	0.00	9781.14	Unopen

Program - LEARN   Status Date: 12/31/1997

WP	Description	BCWS	BCWS	ACWP	BAC	Status
01	Fuselage	0.00	0.00	0.00	14987.50	Unopen
02	Wings	0.00	0.00	0.00	9582.39	Unopen
03	Interior	0.00	0.00	0.00	13161.98	Unopen

Add.   Delete   Details   Close   Help

Figure 8.1   The basic input screen for *Cobra*. Note the requirement to define both the WBS and OBS in the upper part of the screen – these are the cost accounts. Selecting a cost account will reveal the associated work packages in the lower part. This clearly reflects the intended compliance with DODI 7000.2 requirements

accounting system. Work packages need both a value content comprised of either a labour element given in time units (hours) and/or a pure cost (materials and purchases), plus start and finish dates. To this limited extent, *Cobra* contains the time-phased plan but no logic is included to link the time relationship of one work package with any other, hence the plan cannot be analysed for its properties nor will a change in any particular work package's dates reflect itself on any future or linked packages.

As most projects will be planned using a conventional project planning package, *Cobra* incorporates an 'Integration Wizard'. This feature connects directly to either *Open Plan, Primavera Project Planner* or *Microsoft Project* to pick up schedule date information. In addition the Integration Wizard can pick up more data: specifically work breakdown structures, resource definitions and charge rates from the planning software if the fields are defined to it. Time-phased budgets are obtained from the activities to which resources have been assigned; activity status information can also be obtained directly from the planning tool.

Budgeted Costs for Work Scheduled are calculated automatically from the defined work contents and overheads, but when it comes to calculating the earned value (BCWP), there is a choice of methods (% complete, 50% at start, 50% at finish, etc), and each work package must have one method specified. Entering a date for 'time now' will cause the BCWSs to be calculated. Giving each work package a status of either 'opened' or 'complete' will allow the calculation of earned values based on the chosen method. To complete the calculation, Actual Costs of Work Performed need to be obtained from the accounting system and entered either manually or by computerized means. This requires the accounting system to use the same coding structure as *Cobra*. Unlike most other planning systems, *Cobra* is able to make a forecast of where things might end if the trends to date are continued. Using the BCWP, BCWS and ACWP figures, nine alternative methods are available depending on which groups of figures (such as current value, three-month average or cumulative to date) are used to calculate the performance indices. Figure 8.2 gives an example of a forecast report.

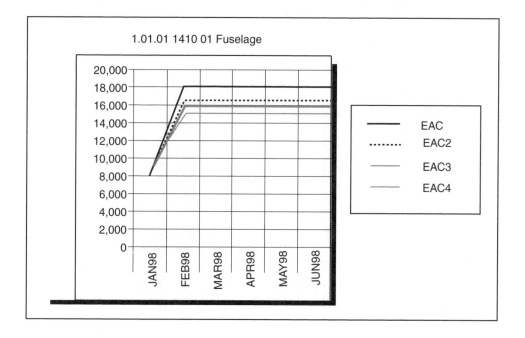

Figure 8.2   Four different forecasting methods have been used to estimate the final cost (EAC) of work package No. 1.01.01 1410 01. There is considerable difference in the results

Figure 8.3 shows a Cost Performance Report (CPR) from *Cobra* which precisely follows the US DoE format. Graphical representations of project progress are also available as shown in Figure 8.4. A large selection of alternative reports is provided and it is possible to create reports to your own requirements.

Beside earned value reporting these specialist packages offer many other features such as:

- trend analysis and forecasting
- report consolidation to increasingly high levels
- multiple project combination reporting
- departmental efficiency calculation
- tracking of schedule and budget revisions
- proposal pricing
- currency cost conversion.

For large projects involving extensive accounting and cost reporting requirements, these specialist packages should be considered.

Cost Performance Report - Work Breakdown Structure

Contractor:	Welcom Software Technology			Contract Type/No: FFP	A001	Project Name/No: Flight Control			Report Period: 31/12/01	
Location:	15995 N. Barkers Landing									

Quantity	Negotiated Cost	Est. Cost Authorized Unpriced Work	Tgt. Profit/Fee %	Tgt. Price	Est Price	Share Ratio	Contract Ceiling	Estimated Contract Ceiling	31/1/02
1	110,000	0	10,450 / 10	120,450	120,450	0	120,450	120,450	

	Current Period					Cumulative to Date					At Completion		
WBS(3)	Budget Cost		Actual Cost	Variance		Budget Cost		Actual Cost	Variance			Latest Revised	
Item	Work Scheduled	Work Performed	Work Performed	Schedule	Cost	Work Scheduled	Work Performed	Work Performed	Schedule	Cost	Budgeted	Estimate	Variance
(1)	(1)	(2)	(3)	(4)	(5)	(6)	(7)	(8)	(9)	(10)	(11)	(12)	(13)
1.01.01 Frame Design	8,938	8,938	11,688	0	-2,750	8,938	8,938	11,688	0	-2,750	33,528	36,278	-2,750
1.01.03 Flight Control	0	0	0	0	0	0	0	0	0	0	28,714	26,714	0
1.02.02 Flight Simulation	0	0	0	0	0	0	0	0	0	0	11,593	11,593	0
1.03.01 Experiment Design	0	0	0	0	0	0	0	0	0	0	3,488	3,488	0
1.04.03 Test Prototype	0	0	0	0	0	0	0	0	0	0	4,650	4,650	0
1.05.02 Project Management	688	688	688	0	0	688	688	688	0	0	8,505	8,505	0
Gen. and Admin.	1,031	1,031	1,403	0	-371	1,031	1,031	1,403	0	-371	9,110	9,481	-371
Undist. Budget											0	0	0
Sub Total	10,656	10,656	13,778	0	-3,121	10,656	10,656	13,778	0	-3,121	99,588	102,709	-3,121
Management Resrv.											10,412	0	10,412
Total	10,656	10,656	13,778	0	-3,121	10,656	10,656	13,778	0	-3,121	110,000	102,709	7,291

Figure 8.3   Cost Performance Report (CPR) generated by *Cobra*. The format follows that defined on C-spec DODI 7000. 10: Contract Cost Performance, Funds Status and Cost/Schedule Status Report

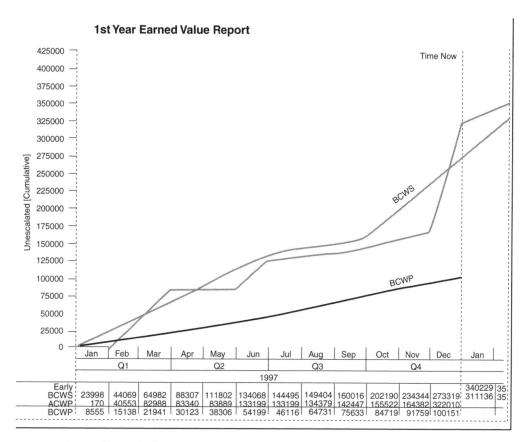

1st Year Earned Value Report

	Jan	Feb	Mar	Apr	May	Jun	Jul	Aug	Sep	Oct	Nov	Dec	Jan	
Early BCWS	23998	44069	64982	88307	111802	134068	144495	149404	160016	202190	234344	273319	340229	35
													311136	35
ACWP	170	40553	82988	83340	83889	133199	133199	134379	142447	155522	164382	322010		
BCWP	8555	15138	21941	30123	38306	54199	46116	64731	75633	84719	91759	100151		

Figure 8.4   Tracking of budget and actual costs over time in *Cobra*

General project planning packages

Whereas stand-alone or specialist earned value packages have tended to conform to the US requirements, earned value calculations are also possible with the better quality project planning packages. *Primavera Project Planner P3* has already been mentioned and is a typical example as it can perform certain earned value calculations and generate some earned value reports without any of the rigid requirements of the more specialist packages. However, the calculations and the report formats are much more limited, but if there is no requirement to conform to DoD-type reporting, they should certainly be considered as they offer a completely integrated approach within one piece of software.

Earned value methods always demanded a time-phased schedule that shows where and when the money is to be spent. From the earliest days of computerized project planning it was realized that adding resource quantities and charge rates to the activities in the plan would generate a time-phased cost schedule and this feature was included. In pure computational terms, adding information to each activity regarding the money actually spent, the amount of progress achieved and performing earned value calculations is comparatively simple; the worked example given in Chapter 3 (see p. 27) shows how straightforward the basic calculations are. However, it was not until the late 1980s that this addition started to become available in project planning packages; by the mid-1990s many packages included an earned value element. This delay probably stems from the fact that throughout the 1970s and 1980s earned value methods were largely confined to US defence and energy contracts and the very special data structure and reporting formats that were demanded could not easily be made compatible with a general purpose planning package. As interest in earned value had not spread outside the defence community, I can only speculate that the software developers saw little point in including these features.

Planning packages exist to schedule tasks in time and generate criticalities, floats and other information about each activity or group of activities. In all cases the key element of data is the activity number as this is the unique identifier for all information about that activity: the quantity of resources, the duration, the day it started, etc. To update the plan, information must be entered at activity level. Remember that in the original DoD specification the plan was excluded from the data set, which instead laid emphasis on the work breakdown structure and the organization structure. This in turn promoted the idea of cost reporting against work breakdown or cost (control) account codes rather than activity numbers, which tended to mean that project plans could not be updated from the costing or time-sheet systems, as reporting was in an incompatible format. If, instead, the activity number is used as the key code for project reporting, earned value calculations become possible within the planning system, but work breakdown or cost (control) account codes become sort-codes rather than reporting/input codes.

The use of a standard planning package to perform earned value calculations is illustrated in Figure 8.5, which is a report prepared by *Primavera Project Planner P3*. Notice that progress and cost information is given for every activity and that progress must be reported by indicating the percentage completion of each activity. Notice also that both resource codes and cost account numbers are also shown but they are not unique to any activity; for example, Resource code TESTMGR relates to activities A2DE1002, ATDE1002, M2AN0658, MNAN0658 and MNAN2707. In order to establish the earned value information, both actual cost and progress must be entered against each activity; as far as the individuals working on the project are concerned, the activity number is the figure to be entered on the time-sheet, not the cost account number. When this is done the data can be sorted by cost account number or resource code. In Figure 8.5, this has been done by cost account number and it can be seen that the complete position of cost account no. 4000 is given. Examination of the total line shows that this account is running well ahead of schedule but at slightly increased cost (CPI = 7442.86/7545.86 = .986). If required, the total project can be summed for all its cost accounts to give the overall project position. Besides the cost account numbers, the system can assign work breakdown structure codes to activities and these work as sort-codes in the same way as the cost account codes. Note the basic similarity of this report to the one generated by *Prestige PC* shown in Figure 2.1 (see p. 16); these two systems are similar in concept and, not surprisingly, there is a similarity in their treatment of earned value.

This system contains both work breakdown structure codes and cost account codes plus the ability to provide total cost and basic earned value data for every cost account in the system. This is the reason why systems like *Cobra* can interlink with systems like *Primavera Project Planner*, transfer data, perform further earned value analyses and generate forecasts. Although this system can perform simple earned value calculations it is clearly much less sophisticated than a system like *Cobra* in terms of the reports that it can produce and its ability to generate graphs and forecasts. It might, however, be all that is required to provide the necessary project control, particularly if the project is commercial in nature rather than being done to any government requirements.

TSNS Financial Institution

PRIMAVERA PROJECT PLANNER

Active IS Development Projects

REPORT DATE   8MAR96   RUN NO.   727
14:48

EARNED VALUE REPORT - QUANTITY

START DATE 10JUL95   FIN DATE   9JAN97

Earned Value Report for Programmers & Testers

DATA DATE   28AUG95   PAGE NO.   12

COST ACCOUNT	RESOURCE	ACTIVITY ID	PCT CMS	CUMULATIVE TO DATE			VARIANCE		AT COMPLETION	
				ACWP	BCWP	BCWS	COST	SCHEDULE	BUDGET	ESTIMATE
4000	N TESTMGR	A2DE1002	100.0	24.00	24.00	.00	.00	24.00	24.00	24.00
4000	N TESTMGR	ATDE1002	100.0	24.00	24.00	.00	.00	24.00	24.00	24.00
4000	N TESTMGR	M2AN0658	.0	.00	.00	.00	.00	.00	96.00	96.00
4000	N TESTMGR	MNAN0658	100.0	96.00	96.00	96.00	.00	.00	96.00	96.00
4000	N TESTMGR	MNAN0707	.0	.00	.00	7.38	.00	-7.38	8.00	152.00
4000	N TESTQA	A2AN0409	100.0	880.00	880.00	.00	.00	880.00	880.00	880.00
4000	N TESTQA	A2TE0527	100.0	72.00	72.00	.00	.00	72.00	72.00	72.00
4000	N TESTQA	A2TE0717	100.0	24.00	24.00	.00	.00	24.00	24.00	24.00
4000	N TESTQA	A2TE1038	100.0	24.00	24.00	.00	.00	24.00	24.00	24.00
4000	N TESTQA	ATAN0409	100.0	880.00	880.00	.00	.00	880.00	880.00	880.00
4000	N TESTQA	ATTE0527	100.0	72.00	72.00	.00	.00	72.00	72.00	72.00
4000	N TESTQA	ATTE0717	100.0	24.00	24.00	.00	.00	24.00	24.00	24.00
4000	N TESTQA	ATTE1038	100.0	24.00	24.00	.00	.00	24.00	24.00	24.00
4000	N TESTQA	C2TE2817	.0	.00	.00	.00	.00	.00	128.00	128.00
4000	N TESTQA	CSTE2817	.0	.00	.00	.00	.00	.00	64.00	64.00
4000	N TESTQA	RPTE1852	.0	.00	.00	.00	.00	.00	144.00	144.00
	TEST*	TOTAL	38.5	7574.86	7442.86	1259.32	-132.00	6183.54	19320.00	19846.86

Figure 8.5   Earned value report from *Primavera Project Planner P3*. This example shows the final sheet of a 12-sheet report. Notice that there is a large positive schedule variance indicating that this block of work is running well ahead of schedule, as can be seen from the large number of activities that are shown as 100% complete against a BCWS of zero which indicates that they are not yet planned to start. What is missing from this report is the reason for this situation

Contact details for the software mentioned in this chapter are given below

Product title	Vendor	Tel/Fax	Web site

Artemis
  Cost View
  Project View
	International
	Corporation Ltd
	261 Bath Road
	Slough
	Berks SL1 4DX
		Tel
		(44) 01753 727100
		
		Fax
		(44) 01753 727099
			www.artemispm.com

	Artemis International Solutions Corp. 4041 MacArthur Boulevard Suite 260 Newport Beach California 92660	Tel (01) 800 477 6648 Fax (01) 949 660 7020	
Microsoft Project	Microsoft Ltd Microsoft Campus Thames Valley Park Reading RG6 1WG	Tel (44)0870 60 10 100 Fax (44) 0870 6010 200	www.microsoft.com
OpenPlan Professional OpenPlan Desktop	Welcom UK 26/28 Church Road Welwyn Garden City Herts AL8 6PW	Tel (44) 01707 331231 Fax (44) 01707 330187	www.welcom.com
Cobra	Welcom 15995 N. Barkers Landing Rd Suite 350 Houston Texas TX 77079	Tel (01) 281 558 0514 Fax (01) 281 584 7828	
Pimavera Project Planner	Primavera Systems Inc. Second floor, Commonwealth House 2 Chalkhill Road London W6 8DW	Tel (44) 020 8563 5500 Fax (44) 020 8563 5533	www.primavera.com
	Primavera Systems Inc. Three Bala Plaza West Suite 700 Bala Cynwyd PA 19004	Tel (01) 610 667 8600 Fax (01) 610 667 7894	

9 Implementing Earned Value Methods

Earned value performance measurement is no different to any other tool, it needs to be used properly if it is to be effective; use it wrongly and it may be more trouble than it is worth. To make it work successfully in any project organization, two major categories of elements must exist:

- **Systems elements**
  - a time-based plan with a full costing
  - a work breakdown structure allied to the plan
  - a work authorization process
  - a data collection system
  - a method of assessing and reporting progress
  - a suitable accounting process
  - a report generating system
  - a change control procedure

- **Managerial elements**
  - an organization with a responsibility/work matrix or similar arrangement by which staff are responsible and accountable for progress on their assigned work
  - the right culture; most importantly acceptance by the project staff and the backing of senior management.

An activity network forms the ideal medium for the time-based plan; it is well understood as a project management technique and can be handled by any project planning package. Suitable software is available at prices to suit all types of project; furthermore, most project planning packages have the ability to accept resources and charge rates onto planned activities and from there produce both resource loadings and costings. Comprehensive systems will allow costs to be directly enterable to cover purchases of services and materials. Whatever system is used, it must be capable of producing total costs against individual activities that are phased to reflect the plan. Those costs should be capable of being summarized upwards and they should have a fixed relationship to the work breakdown structure, if a formalized WBS is being used.

Although using a work breakdown structure is not an absolute requirement in order to perform earned value calculations, rationalizing the work into a recognizable structure does help with both reporting and control and it is to be recommended. Work breakdown structures tend to exist in one form or another in most companies and projects; they may not be recognized as such but they often appear in the form of 'cost codes' that are used for time and cost bookings; any rational coding system represents some form of work structuring.

What may be absent is the formality and type of structuring needed by earned value methods. If rational or useful data structuring is not present then this issue needs to be addressed; whatever structure is devised it must conform to the requirements of the project and the limitations of the data gathering systems in use within the organization.

Work must proceed in an orderly way and the managerial process must include a way of formally authorizing work to start. This need not be a major restriction on the project's activities as ultimately all the work is (or should be) under the project manager's control, but without a proper system of authorization, work could start in an out-of-sequence fashion which could lead to nugatory work that may need to be altered or repeated later in the project, or to budgetary problems if there are cash flow limitations.

The data collection system is absolutely fundamental to the efficient working of earned value methods. All organizations that are commercial in nature have mechanisms for gathering data about their costs but the issue is whether the data is sufficiently detailed and timely. In most companies that are sited in one place, basic data about project costs can be obtained through the time bookings and purchase accounting systems as these are fundamental to commercial operations associated with projects. This data may be less easy to compile in more transient project organizations, for which special arrangements might have to be made.

The method of assessing progress for earned value measurement is likely to require a new discipline that must be maintained, ideally it should be linked to the responsibility/authority structure. Those responsible for the success or completion of specific tasks should be required to report progress and be accountable for achievement.

Earned value methods were founded on the idea of cost as a common denominator that linked all elements of a project, hence an accounting system that is accurate, timely and capable of taking basic progress and other project data and turning it into costs associated with defined activities or work packages is essential.

None of the above will mean anything if the information cannot be turned into meaningful results that can reported for managerial action. The earned value method is a highly prescriptive, mathematically based method of recording progress; it demands very specific data to be reported. Although there is no absolute requirement for a computerized system to do the work, in practice it would be difficult for anything but the most straightforward projects. With projects involving thousands of activities, a computerized approach is essential in today's environment where staff costs are comparatively high. Choice of suitable software is a significant issue and some of the options are covered in Chapter 8.

Projects, particularly advanced technology or innovative ones, are inherently unstable. It is part of the job of the project manager to bring stability and order; successful project managers can do this with the right procedures, adequate resources and a competent team. Uncontrolled changes lead to an unstable situation, hence they should, as far as is possible, be restricted to the absolute minimum. When changes are necessary they should be properly considered before being formally incorporated in the plan with all the required budget and contractual changes.

The right type of organization structure needs to be created in which staff with the appropriate authority are made responsible for progress and direction and are accountable for what has been accomplished. If people in authority are unwilling to accept responsibility, then any form of managerial control is going to fail. If this is the case, the problem could, in a few instances, lie with particular individuals but in the majority of cases the problem is likely to lie with the organization itself. The causes can be many but they could include:

- Actual authority over resources or actions is not matched to the implied responsibility.
- There is no input to setting the objectives or task goals.
- The objectives or task goals are perceived as unrealistic.
- The objectives or task goals are unclear or poorly defined.
- The plan, as set out, is considered unworkable.
- Too many outside influences over which there is no control could determine the outcome.
- Too much stigma or heavy penalties are associated with failure.

Whatever the cause, if evasion of responsibility is perceived it is likely to be symptomatic of some other failure which needs to be properly diagnosed and addressed.

The earned value methods with the associated disciplines and systems must be accepted by the project team, who will have to cooperate in its workings; if they do not, for whatever reason, it will fail. Ultimately, the whole system must have backing at the most senior level if it is to succeed; top management must endorse the procurement and installation of whatever systems are required and they must be seen to take an active interest in the reports and projections that come from it. If it is perceived that top management are not really interested but are simply paying lip-service to fashion or customer wishes and see the whole process as a distraction, then the system will gradually fall into disuse as the incentive to maintain the required discipline is not there.

Any organization contemplating introducing earned value methods should consider all the above points and take steps to see that all have been adequately addressed. If any are neglected then installing and using earned value will be difficult, if not impossible; what results are produced will be of doubtful value and are likely to be disregarded.

Personnel aspects associated with earned value methods

It is probably true to say that many if not most organizations that have implemented earned value methods have not found the process either simple or straightforward. Difficulties can arise both from technical aspects including the procedures, the software, the data gathering or the management of the data set, and from the staff associated with the project.

The technical aspects have already been mentioned in earlier chapters and it comes down to the individual organizations to chose systems and procedures appropriate to the needs of their projects; for this a thorough examination of both the project and the organizational requirements, plus a study of available products, is essential.

For many staff working in the development field, earned value performance measurement will come as something of a shock. There can be little doubt that, upon its introduction, there will be resistance from some quarters, particularly from those members of the project staff that have not been used to any form of performance monitoring. It may also come from project managers who may feel that a technique that exposes potential cost or schedule overruns to demanding or unsympathetic senior management at an early point in the project could be damaging to their own prospects. This resistance is understandable, particularly with complex or innovative work where there is always an element of the unknown and people cannot be expected to meet and solve unknown problems within fixed time and cost parameters. However reasonable this proposition may seem, the business world, in general, is finding it increasingly difficult to take that view and there is a growing insistence on the part of customer organizations for fixed price development contracts with closely defined technical objectives. The underlying reason for this is a desire to shift the effects of cost, schedule and technical risks from the sponsor to the contractor. The traditional response to uncertainty, in a fixed price situation, is to put in large contingencies, both in time and cost, but this becomes more difficult in the context of competition. It becomes imperative that industry should pay closer attention to both the initial estimating and the control that is exercised while the project is underway. Departmental managers must become more responsible for the value generated by their departments and performance measurement is probably the only way it can be done.

Difficulties with staff can be expected: the three quotations are given below regarding problems with the project staff are taken from a survey of earned value in the United Kingdom in 1994:[1]

[We have not achieved] buy-in to the system from every-one. [There is] unwillingness to change work practices, [a] not-invented-here syndrome [and people] don't want to be accountable for [their] work.

Not all the staff have signed on to the concept. The system shows efficiency against original budgets. In the early stages low efficiencies were achieved, due to inaccurate budget levels but staff saw this as a reflection on their work.

Its implementation suffered from a lack of education and training support and there was unwillingness to adopt required new working practices to go with the discipline which the tool imposed.

It is important to ensure the full cooperation of all concerned. A 'hearts and minds' campaign, together with education and training, will be necessary and it must be seen to be effectively backed by senior management. Performance measurement must not be seen to be a threat, although some will see it that way, as this contributor to the survey indicates:

Resistance was driven by the fear of change and the desire to preserve the status quo, particularly by those who stood to lose control over the content and release of information. Forms of resistance ranged from any perceived deficiency that could be found, through constant questioning of the tool selection process and the need for and applicability of the new project management system.

The use of earned value techniques opens up the details of the project for scrutiny in a way that no other system does and that can lead to real insecurity. For those that have been used to managing by throwing a 'cloak of secrecy' around the project or creating deliberately vague or imprecise reports, earned value methods can be a real threat. One of the most favoured techniques is to hide behind the slowness or imprecision in the company's accounting system as a way of obscuring the true picture. Another is to keep revising the plan so that all reports are essentially history that can't really be tied to anything concrete.

The majority of people want to do a good and valuable job; performance measurement actually reveals the value of their efforts in a way that has not previously been so clear. It also provides warning signals about things going wrong; usually something can be done about a difficult situation, providing it is recognized early enough. These are positive benefits but they need to be sold to the staff, commitment is all important. It must be pointed out that every member of a company is a stakeholder in its future for it is the company's future that holds the key to their own prosperity. The continued presence of any company in the marketplace is totally dependent on providing the customers with what they want at a price they can afford and that implies giving value for money. The earned value concept is aimed directly at the 'value for money' objective.

Getting started

If earned value performance measurement is to be implemented, the decision should, ideally, be taken at the outset of the project and incorporated in the planning and control arrangements. It can be implemented at a mid-point in a project but that can be difficult and time-consuming. Managers submitting estimates must be persuaded to thoroughly scrutinize the project plan and the technical specification to ensure a full understanding of what is expected and its implications. Undue pressure for low estimates should not be applied. Planning engineers should also ensure that adequate time is allowed for each activity. Resource demands should be approved by senior management for it is they who will be tasked with ensuring that resources in terms of staff, materials and money will be made available when required. In simple terms, a new and more formalized arrangement will exist between all the parties. Departmental managers must be made responsible for their budgets and this must be clearly understood in their relationship with the project manager.

Reporting systems must be set up to gather the cost and progess data. The generation of regular performance reports is vital; responsible managers must see how they are doing at regular and well-defined points. It must be made clear that progress assessments will be required for each work package and the responsible managers must submit their reports on time. Project management staff responsible for operating the system must set up a regular routine for themselves and must ensure that authorizations go out on time and that managers know when progress assessments are needed.

Undoubtedly one of the most important aspects of implementation is the education and training of the project staff. Earned value performance measurement is a methodology in its own right; it is not an intuitive process. People can easily get confused and it has acquired a history of its own with all the attendant baggage. The latter aspect includes a reputation for being bureaucratic and generally applicable to the larger type of project that can absorb the associated costs. Furthermore, a considerable US-inspired jargon has evolved with a large number of unfamiliar terms and acronyms as well as some tightly defined budgeting and reporting requirements. All of this can be very off-putting, implying a kind of built-in rigidity that the conventional wisdom associated with earned value management does nothing to dispel. It is not difficult to see how staff can question the need for procedures they may see as marginal to the main thrust of getting the project tasks completed. As the quotations above show, it is easy for staff to become both suspicious and fearful of the discipline and the performance measurements aspect.

Proper education about the whole subject of earned value performance measurement needs to be made a significant part of the implementation process. The reasons for this are twofold: first, people must know what the special terms mean and what the procedures are in order to provide the right information to make the whole system work; second, they must know what the outputs are, how to understand them and how they can help in the management of the project, so that unjustified fears and resistance can be replaced by a more enlightened view. Few people engaged on project work will ever come to love earned value, unless they happen to make a living out of it, but people can certainly learn to live with it, accept it for what it is and appreciate the benefits it can bring. Two quotations from the survey reinforce the message:

If the project team do not buy-in to the products of the system they tend to be discounted and pro-active dealing with risks is reduced.

I would spend more time explaining to staff why we are using the system and the benefits it has to us.

Perhaps the most important point of all about implementing and using earned value performance measurement is to see it as a process that is essentially adaptable to individual project circumstances. Its widespread adoption across the general field of project management in the United Kingdom and elsewhere outside the USA was undoubtedly hampered by the rigid methodology that was often seen to accompany it whenever any serious descriptions of the process appeared. This, as we have seen, stemmed from its US Department of Defense origins that tended to stamp an official 'correctness' on a particular way of working that many saw as overly bureaucratic and inappropriate to their own project circumstances. The specialist software tools tended to confirm this view. Many project managers were right to reject earned value in the way it had been prescribed, but it is possible to take a more tailored approach that chooses those aspects that are relevant while avoiding other aspects that are marginal. The ending of the old C/SCSC regime in the USA has perhaps signalled to the world that there is a more flexible approach which can give all the benefits of performance measurement that concentrates on results and usefulness rather than rigid procedures.

Other issues can arise from the introduction of earned value methods, in particular the use to which the performance measurement results can be put. For example, problems can arise for the individual team members if low performance indicators are viewed as a reflection on their work. This interpretation could be used by unscrupulous managers as a stick to wield over the team, but it may be completely unjustified and lead to a loss of cooperation or a collapse in morale.

In addition, contractual arrangements can be put under strain, particularly where fixed price contracts are involved. Earned value methods were devised in an era when cost-plus-fee contracting was the norm; contractors were paid according to the bills they incurred thus reporting the ACWP was consistent with this practice. Where a fixed-price arrangement is in operation, some contractors have refused to make actual cost data available as this is now considered to be commercially confidential. The argument is that as the cost risk is now being borne by the contractor there is no reason to disclose information that could, if the contractor is seen to do the work significantly more cheaply than quoted, leave him open to charges of making excess profits. The quotations below show some of the problems:

Some of the more senior staff did not believe that the reports and efficiency graphs should be submitted to the client even though the company had signed a contract saying that it would.

They [the contractors] perceive they are on a 'price' and will manage accordingly, [hence] reluctance to reveal cost information.

Earned value methods belong to a time when it was normal for sponsors to bear the cost risks associated with projects but current practice is increasingly shifting the risks onto the contractor where these methods may not sit so easily. From the sponsor's point of view, in a fixed price situation with no variations, the ACWP will always equal the claimed BCWP and the cost performance index will be 1.0. as all the cost risks are transferred to the contractor. From a contractor's viewpoint, there could well be merit in maintaining an earned value measurement system for internal use as it can generate important information with respect to progress against the requirements of the project and the anticipated profits. However, much of this data might be viewed as commercially sensitive and not to be disclosed to the sponsor, a view with which one has to sympathize given the shift in the risk aspect from the sponsor to the contractor. Even in a fixed price contract situation, all sponsors have a right to be informed of schedule progress as this could affect other related activities on the project.

Using fixed price contracts is a very direct form of cost control but it is one that is exercised through the contracting process and the transference of risk rather than through the demands of the reporting system and the accounting procedure. It must be recognized that in this situation there is an element of conflict between the demands for openness on the part of the sponsor and the equally valid requirements for confidentiality on the part of contractors. Ultimately it is for the two parties to the contract to agree what information will be made available; there may be no hard and fast rules about this – it may just come down to what is acceptable in the circumstances.

None of this should imply that earned value performance measurement could not be employed on a project that used fixed price contracts. Baseline plans can still be agreed, variation orders can still be made out to cover changes, and contingencies can still be drawn upon. Performance reports can still be required from the participants but aspects of the actual costs incurred by the contractors may be hidden. Ultimately this may not be of great concern to the sponsor; as far as he is concerned the actual costs are those contained on the invoices from the contractors. Fixed price contracting simply increases the degree of confidence about what the value of those invoices will be.

Perspective

Earned value principles have been around for over forty years but during the first thirty the application was largely confined to the US defence and energy community. The advent of affordable PC-based project planning software with earned value features has brought the method to the project community on a much wider scale, but its application is still not a general feature of project management in the way that network-based planning packages are used.

Earned value was born in a highly disciplined environment with complex projects procured under very exacting contract conditions by a sponsor with an army of administrators to ensure compliance. Despite the fact that many of the projects to which the method was applied were highly innovative and subject to frequent changes and delays, the basic assumption was of a well perceived future with few changes against which actual progress could be measured with precision. This is rarely the case hence one of the principal assumptions has always had a somewhat shaky foundation. Acceptance of the need for change is found in the procedures for baseline revision but the more frequently this has to be invoked the less valid any inferences from earned value measurements become.

This implies that earned value methods are more suited to projects with a well-perceived plan at the outset. Where the project is one in which the later activities are dependent on the outcome of earlier ones, the baseline plan cannot be seen with clarity. This fact was recognized by the adoption, on large development projects, of a procedure for breaking major projects into discrete phases, each of which would be costed and managed in its own right; at the end of each phase there is an opportunity either to stop the project with no further liabilities, or to continue. During one phase enough work would be done to ensure that many of the technical risks were removed and the next phase could be planned with reasonable detail; hence a decision to proceed could be taken with a high degree of confidence in the outcome.

Other types of project may find earned value of less use because there are significant difficulties in estimating the work content if much of it consists of research and experimentation. Drug development is one such type of project where ethical and safety issues come into play; ultimately these are far more important issues than cost and schedule matters and can have a major bearing on the course and duration of the project.

Earned value assumes an ordered world of well-defined and measurable quantities, in terms of both time and cost. However, the advent of risk analysis techniques over the last ten years has shifted the emphasis to the uncertain and the variable. It may be a more sophisticated view of the real world, where things are expressed in terms of probabilities, but often it does not make things easier to manage. The probabilistic view certainly does not sit easily with the concept of a fixed baseline, but project management has always been a pragmatic discipline that can embrace potential conflicts and make the best of what is available.

On the basis of the survey, the experience of companies that have implemented earned value performance measurement is that of a qualified success, but a success nevertheless. The majority of those surveyed said their experience in one area of activity would encourage them to make it a company-wide or project-wide process. None was contemplating abandoning the approach having got it to work, even if they had encountered problems.

Two basic problems emerged: first, that of staff commitment and second, the appropriateness and detail generated in the reports. If staff do not fully understand and subscribe to the system objectives, resistance will be met and exacerbated by lack of proper education. The level and appropriateness of the reporting arrangement needs careful thought. Too much detail can demand large amounts of clerical effort that may be seen as costly. Large amounts of detail that are not easily summarized upwards can leave the picture unclear and management may be left with no obvious choices of action as the messages are too obscure. When that happens the worth of the entire process can be called into question as management revert to other methods that seem to provide the information they want. Whether those other methods really provide any better information is not really the issue, what tends to be favoured in real project management situations is what is convenient, available, understandable and is acceptable within the politics of the project. Earned value specialists, take note!

Although earned value methods have many strengths and advantages for project management, they also have certain weaknesses, some of which have already been indicated. Perhaps the biggest of all is that earned value methods can measure current performance and indicate future trends, but if those trends indicate trouble ahead, earned value gives no clue as to what to do about it. Although earned value methods may indicate where the problem is, they don't say what it is. Other techniques within project management are rather more helpful. For example, Value Engineering contains a methodology that will lead to improved value products, Risk Analysis contains such methods as decision theory which, if followed, should lead to the best decisions, while Network Analysis can identify the critical path and the subcritical activities and thus the overall duration. Earned value methods remain completely silent when it comes to what actions to take because they contain no inherent method of problem solving; cost and schedule difficulties are rarely the cause in themselves but are symptoms of other more fundamental problems.

Earned value performance measurement should be viewed as a useful tool for the project manager that complements all the other tools in the set but does not replace any of them. All the other skills and disciplines, both technical and human, are still necessary but better information should result in improved decision making and a better-informed team. Together they should lead to better overall project performance, which is the holy grail.

Note

1. Webb, Alan (1995) 'Integrated cost and schedule control – a survey of UK experience', The *Engineering Management Journal*, Vol. 5, No. 3, June.

1 *Terms Used Within Earned Value Methods*

The terms given below are those that are commonly used in the discussion and use of earned value methods within the general field of project management. Many were first coined in the context of US government contracting practice and their original definitions reflected that fact. However, some of the terms are now widely used in other non-US contexts in which their original definitions are not so appropriate; the definitions below are for general interpretation, explanation and guidance rather than the original definitions.

Actual Cost of Work Performed (ACWP) – The total actual expenditure for any activity, purchase, project or part of a project at a point in time, the Actual Cost (AC).

ANSI/EIA-748-1998 – A US commercial standard for guidelines for implementing Earned Value Management Systems on projects; it is now applied to US government contracts as well as commercial enterprises.

Apportioned effort (AE) – A method of distributing earned value to activities whose progress is governed by another activity, by taking a value that is directly proportional to the value earned on the related activity.

Authorization To Proceed (ATP) – A formal instruction to start work on a task.

Authorized work – The work for which authority to proceed has been given; in an earned value situation this implies that a budget has been approved for it and it is contained within the project plan.

Authorized, Unpriced Work (AUW) – The authorized work for which no definite budget has been set. This is typically due to negotiations not being completed on contract changes.

Baseline plan – An agreed plan against which all changes will be recorded and all progress and costs will be measured.

Budget – An amount of money authorized or agreed to cover a defined amount of work or purchases.

Budget at Completion (BAC) – The sum of all planned project costs plus any contingency for management reserve.

Budgeted Cost for Work Performed (BCWP) – The total planned cost associated with the completed work or acquired purchase on any activity, purchase, project or part of a project at a point in time: the Earned Value (EV).

Budgeted Cost for Work Scheduled (BCWS) – The total planned cost for any activity, purchase, project or part of a project scheduled to be achieved by a given point in time: the Planned Value (PV).

C-Spec – Abbreviation for the US government's C/SCSC project control procedure. Now an outdated term.

Comprehensive Estimated Cost at Completion (CEAC) – An all-embracing estimate of costs at completion, often associated with a complete revision of the baseline programme.

Contingency (cost) – A sum of money set aside or provided to cover unforeseen expenditure.

Contingency (time) – An amount of time contained within a project plan to allow for a schedule overrun.

Contract Budget Base (CBB) – In a contracted situation: the estimate of the overall contract budget made up of the contract target cost plus an estimate of the authorized, but unpriced, work.

Contract price – In a contracted situation: the price payable by the customer under the terms of the contract for the properly delivered goods and services contained within the contract scope.

Contract Target Cost (CTC) – In a contracted situation: the sum of the authorized and priced work but excluding the estimated cost of any authorized, unpriced changes.

Contract Target Price (CTP) – In a contracted situation: the negotiated estimated cost (CTC) plus profit or fee.

Contract Work Breakdown Structure (CWBS) – The work breakdown structure as contractually agreed between the parties (often product based).

Contractor – One who performs work on behalf of another on the basis of a legally binding agreement.

Control account (formerly **Cost account**) – A budget account associated with a work breakdown structure element, at which lower-level tasks are gathered for the purposes of managerial control and specifically assigned to one element within the organization structure.

Control account manager – One who is responsible for the costs and progress associated with a control account.

Cost Performance Index (CPI) – The rate at which value is earned for the actual costs incurred, it equates to the BCWP divided by the ACWP. Also called the cost efficiency.

Cost Performance Report (CPR) – A US DoD defined report format for reporting cost and schedule progress data for contracts that require EVMS compliance.

Cost-plus-fee contract, Cost-plus contract – A contractual arrangement in which the contractor is reimbursed for his actual incurred costs plus an additional fee for profit. Also called a 'Cost reimbursable' contract.

Cost/Schedule Status Report (C/SSR) – A US DoD-defined report format for reporting cost and schedule progress data for contracts that do not meet the threshold for EVMS compliance (a simpler report than the CPR).

Cost Variance (CV) – In the context of earned value reporting: the arithmetic difference between the earned value (BCWP) and the actual cost (ACWP) on any activity, purchase, project or part of a project at a point in time.
    Not in the context of earned value reporting: the arithmetic difference between the planned cost (BCWS) and the actual cost (ACWP) on any activity, purchase, project or part of a project at a point in time.

C/SCSC – Acronym for Cost/Schedule Control Systems Criteria, a US Department of Defense procedure for project management incorporating earned value methods, used for assessing and ensuring contractor compliance with a set methodology. Also known as C-Spec, no longer in use.

DODI 7000.2 – A US Department of Defense Instruction (1967) for project management on major acquisition projects incorporating the Cost/Schedule Control Systems Criteria, superseded by DoD 5000. 2R.

DOD 5000.2R – A US Department of Defense Instruction (1996), containing in Part II Section B the earned value management systems guidelines.

Earned Value – The value attached to that which has been achieved on any activity, purchase, part of a project or project in terms of what was planned or expected at the start. Also known as the Budgeted Cost for Work Performed (BCWP).

Earned Value Management Sysems (EVMS) – Project management procedure using earned value principles and implied in US standard ANSI/EIA-748-1998.

Estimate At Completion (EAC) – The sum of all actual costs at a point in time plus all estimated remaining costs to complete a project or part of a project. Also referred to as the Estimated cost at completion.

Estimated cost at completion – Another term for the Estimate At Completion (EAC).

Estimated Time to Completion (ETTC) – An estimate, at a point in time, of the likely overall duration of a project or part of a project.

Estimate to Completion (ETC) – An estimate, at a point in time, of the costs still to be incurred to complete the project or part of a project.

Fixed price contract – A contractual arrangement where a contractor is paid a fixed sum for a defined piece of work irrespective of his actual expenditure.

Incentive contract – A contractual arrangement where the contractor is rewarded with an increased fee if performance above an agreed level is achieved.

Integrated Baseline Review (IBR) – A formal process in which both the sponsor and the contractor examine a baseline plan to establish its completeness, realism and practicality.

Latest Revised Estimate (LRE) – The most recent estimate of the final cost of a project, or part of a project, based on known work. Note, this term is sometimes used interchangeably with the Estimate At Completion (EAC).

Level of Effort (LOE) – A method of costing work which is time dependent rather that associated with any definitive output, for example, support services such as project management or maintaining the project accounts. Value is accrued according to the elapsed time and resources employed rather than observed progress.

Liquidated damages agreement – A contractual arrangemeent that provides for a final, non-negotiable settlement for a loss due to some aspect, other than cost, of non-performance of a contract; it is often applied to lateness in delivery or product performance below that stipulated in the agreed specification.

Management Reserve (MR) – A financial contingency under the direct control of senior management outside the performance measurement baseline.

Original Budget (OB) – The original amount of money provisioned for an activity, purchase, project or part of a project.

Original Duration (OD) – The original planned time over which an activity, project or part of a project should take place.

Organization Structure, Organization Breakdown Structure (OBS) – The logical and hierarchical arrangement of both function and authority of a company engaged on a project.

Over Target Baseline (OTB) – A baseline programme resulting from formal reprogramming, where additional funds over the value of the contract are incorporated into the baseline plan.

Performance Measurement Baseline (PMB) – An agreed programme of work against which progress will be measured which includes all known and planned work; it includes all costs within the Budget at Completion less management reserve.

Prime contractor – A contracting organization with overall responsibility for delivering a project; normally this will involve coordination and control of a group of lower-level contractors.

Project manager – One who is charged with the overall direction of a unique undertaking. This term is sometimes synonymous with program manager or programme manager.

Responsibility Assignment Matrix (RAM) – A matrix showing how control accounts for tasks in the work breakdown structure are assigned to functions within the organization.

Schedule Performance Index (SPI) – The rate of progress against the original schedule with respect to elapsed time (by reference to the earned value). It equates to the BCWP divided by the BCWS at a point in time. Also called schedule efficiency.

Schedule Variance (SV) – The arithmetic difference between the earned value (BCWP) and the planned cost (BCWS) on any activity, purchase, project or part of a project at a point in time.

Sponsor – One who finances a project; he or she may also have a controlling interest.

Statement of Work, Scope of Work (SOW) – A definition of a product, group of products, tasks or services to be procured under a contract; by definition it limits what is to be supplied to that which is contained in the statement.

To-Complete Performance Index for budget (TCPI(BAC)) – At a point in time: the rate of generation of earned value required to complete the project within the budget at completion.

To-Complete Performance Index for schedule (TCPI(OD)) – At a point in time: the rate of schedule progress required to complete the project within the planned overall duration.

Undistributed Budget (UB) – A holding account used to temporarily contain the budget for recently negotiated contract charges until detailed planning can be accomplished.

Variance at Completion (VAC) – An estimate of the likely difference between the planned cost and the actual cost of the project or part of a project when complete. The arithmetic difference between the BAC and the EAC.

Work Breakdown Structure (WBS) – A logical, hierarchical arrangement of the work elements within a project.

Work package – An identifiable, discrete and defined block of work.

Work package manager – One who is responsible for the conduct of the work contained in a work package.

2 Earned Value Management Systems Criteria

In 1996 a set of 32 criteria for the operation of earned value management systems within US companies was produced. This was based on the 35 criteria set out in the DODI 7000.2 instruction for government defence contracts but was intended for more general use. These criteria were later incorporated in an American national commercial standard ANSI/EIA-748-1998 which provides general guidance for the operation of earned value management systems. In 1999 this standard was adopted by the US Department of Defense as the approach to be used for project monitoring and control.

Organization

1 Define the authorized work elements for the program. A work breakdown structure (WBS), tailored for effective internal management control, is commonly used in this process.
2 Identify the program organizational structure including the major subcontractors responsible for accomplishing the authorized work, and define the organizational elements in which work will be planned and controlled.
3 Provide for the integration of the company's planning, scheduling, budgeting, work authorization and cost accumulation processes with each other, and as appropriate, the program work breakdown structure and the program organizational structure.
4 Identify the company organization or function responsible for controlling overhead (indirect costs).
5 Provide for integration of the program work breakdown structure and the program organizational structure in a manner that permits cost and schedule performance measurement by elements of either or both structures as needed.

Planning and Budgeting

6 Schedule the authorized work in a manner which describes the sequence of work and identifies significant task interdependencies required to meet the requirements of the program.
7 Identify physical products, milestones, technical performance goals, or other indicators that will be used to measure progress.
8 Establish and maintain a time-phased budget baseline, at the control account level, against which program performance can be measured. Budget for far-term efforts may be held in higher-level accounts until an appropriate time for allocation at the control

account level. Initial budgets established for performance measurement will be based on either internal management goals or the external customer negotiated target cost, including estimates for authorized but undefinitized work. On government contracts, if an over-target baseline is used for performance measurement reporting purposes, prior notification must be provided to the customer.

9 Establish budgets for authorized work with identification of significant cost elements (labour, material, etc.) as needed for internal management and for control of subcontractors.

10. To the extent it is practical to identify the authorized work in discrete work packages, establish budgets for this work in terms of dollars, hours, or other measurable units. Where the entire control account is not subdivided into work packages, identify the far-term effort in larger planning packages for budget and scheduling purposes.

11 Provide that the sum of all work package budgets plus planning package budgets within a control account equals the control account budget.

12 Identify and control level of effort activity by time-phased budgets established for this purpose. Only that effort which is unmeasurable or for which measurement is impractical may be classified as level of effort.

13 Establish overhead budgets for each significant organizational component of the company for expenses which will become indirect costs. Reflect in the program budgets, at the appropriate level, the amounts in overhead pools that are planned to be allocated to the program as indirect costs.

14 Identify management reserves and undistributed budget.

15 Provide that the program target cost goal is reconciled with the sum of all internal program budgets and management reserves.

Accounting Considerations

16 Record direct costs in a manner consistent with the budgets in a formal system controlled by the general books of account.

17 When a work breakdown structure is used, summarize direct costs from control accounts into the work breakdown structure without allocation of a single control account to two or more work breakdown structure elements.

18 Summarize direct costs from the control accounts into the contractor's organizational elements without allocation of a single control account to two or more organizational elements.

19 Record all indirect costs which will be allocated to the contract.

20 Identify unit costs, equivalent units costs, or lot costs when needed.

21 For EVMS (Earned Value Management System), the material accounting system will provide for:

(1) Accurate cost accumulation and assignment of costs to control accounts in a manner consistent with the budgets using recognized, acceptable, costing techniques.

(2) Cost performance measurement at the point in time most suitable for the category of material involved, but no earlier than the time of progress payments or actual receipt of material.

(3) Full accountability of all material purchased for the program including the residual inventory.

Analysis and Management Reports

22 At least on a monthly basis, generate the following information at the control account and other levels as necessary for management control using actual cost data from, or reconcilable with, the accounting system:
   (1) Comparison of the amount of planned budget and the amount of budget earned for work accomplished. This comparison provides the schedule variance.
   (2) Comparison of the amount of the budget earned the actual (applied where appropriate) direct costs for the same work. This comparison provides the cost variance.

23 Identify, at least monthly, the significant differences between both planned and actual schedule performance and planned and actual cost performance, and provide the reasons for the variances in the detail needed by program management.

24 Identify budgeted and applied (or actual) indirect costs at the level and frequency needed by management for effective control, along with the reasons for any significant variances.

25 Summarize the data elements and associated variances through the program organization and/or work breakdown structure to support management needs and any customer reporting specified in the contract.

26 Implement managerial actions taken as the result of earned value information.

27 Develop revised estimates of cost at completion based on performance to date, commitment values for material, and estimates of future conditions. Compare this information with the performance measurement baseline to identify variances at completion important to company management and any applicable customer reporting requirements including statements of funding requirements.

Revisions and Data Maintenance

28 Incorporate authorized changes in a timely manner, recording the effects of such changes in budgets and schedules. In the directed effort prior to negotiation of a change, base such revisions on the amount estimated and budgeted to the program organizations.

29 Reconcile current budgets to prior budgets in terms of changes to the authorized work and internal replanning in the detail needed by management for effective control.

30 Control retroactive changes to records pertaining to work performed that would change previously reported amounts for actual costs, earned value, or budgets. Adjustments should be made only for correction of errors, routine accounting adjustments, effects of customer- or management-directed changes, or to improve the baseline integrity and accuracy of performance measurement data.

31 Prevent revisions to the program budget except for authorized changes.

32 Document changes to the performance measurement baseline.

3 *Formulae Used for Earned Value Calculations*

Formulae used for Earned Value calculations

- **Cost Variance (CV)**
  $$CV = BCWP - ACWP$$

- **Schedule Variance (SV)**
  $$SV = BCWP - BCWS$$

- **Cost Performance Index (CPI)**   (Cost efficiency)
  $$CPI = \frac{BCWP}{ACWP}$$

- **Schedule Performance Index (SPI)**   (Schedule efficiency)

  $$SPI = \frac{BCWP}{BCWS}$$

- **Estimated Cost At Completion (EAC)** The estimated final cost of the project.

  $$EAC = ACWP + \frac{BAC - BCWP}{CPI}$$

  Where: BAC is the Budgeted Cost At Completion

- **Alternative formulae for the Estimated Cost At Completion**

  $$EAC_1 = ACWP + \frac{BAC - BCWP}{0.5 \times CPI + 0.5 \times SPI}$$

  $$EAC_2 = ACWP + \frac{BAC - BCWP}{CPI \times SPI}$$

- **Estimated Time To Completion (ETTC)** The estimated overall duration of the project.

  $$ETTC = ATE + OD - \frac{(ATE \times SPI)}{SPI}$$

Where: BAC is the Budgeted Cost At Completion
ATE is the Actual Time Expended
OD is the Original Duration
Note: this formula becomes increasingly less reliable as the project approaches completion and fails once the Original Duration is exceeded.

- **Variance at completion (VAC)**

  $VAC = BAC - EAC$

- **Schedule variance as a percentage of the scheduled achievement (SV%)**

  $SV\% = \dfrac{BCWP - BCWS}{BCWS} \times 100$

- **Cost variance as a percentage of the earned value (CV%)**

  $CV\% = \dfrac{BCWP - ACWP}{BCWP} \times 100$

- **Percentage complete at the report point**

  $= \dfrac{BCWP}{BAC} \times 100$

- **Percentage spent at the report point**

  $= \dfrac{ACWP}{BAC} \times 100$

- **Percentage of project to be achieved at the report point**

  $= \dfrac{BCWS}{BAC} \times 100$

- **The 'To-complete Performance Index' for budgeted cost (TCPI(BAC))**

  $TCPI(BAC) = \dfrac{BAC - BCWP}{BAC - ACWP}$

- **The 'To-complete Performance Index' for estimated cost (TCPI(EAC))**

  $TCPI(EAC) = \dfrac{EAC - BCWP}{EAC - ACWP}$

- **The 'To-complete Performance Index' for schedule (TCPI(OD))**

  $TCPI(OD) = \dfrac{BAC - BCWP}{BAC - BCWS}$

Index

The Relationship Manager

The Next Generation of Project Management

Tony Davis and Richard Pharro

Traditionally, project managers have been allocated a project and their role has been to deliver on time, to quality standards and within budget. With hindsight the client only recognises what they really want once the project is delivered – and there is often a gap between expectation and final product. The project management role is now changing and the total impact on the business needs to be addressed more effectively – enter the Relationship Manager.

The true role of the Relationship Manager is to act as an orchestral conductor:

- to go to the client and demonstrate his understanding of the client's short-, medium- and long-term objectives;
- to translate this into a form which the project team can address;
- to receive from the project team a specification of the work to be undertaken, including plans, estimates and schedules, together with detailed work and cost breakdown structures to check that they have really understood what needs to be done and by when – and only when the Relationship Manager is satisfied does he return to the client to sell VALUE.

The Relationship Manager has been written to fill the gap between technical and business aspects of successful project delivery. It provides practical guidance on how to make this new way of working a reality and details the skills and techniques necessary to make a success of the latest developments in project management.

GOWER

The Bid Manager's Handbook

David Nickson

Winning significant business on the right terms is an increasingly complex, challenging and time-consuming task, and a successful bid is a vital part of any business offering its services or products to another. This book will help you to enhance the probability of success in winning bids at the desired margins and to set up and run effectively a bid management team. Aimed at two main groups of readers (sales staff managing multi-disciplinary bid teams, and project and technical managers who find themselves managing a bid to support a sales campaign), *The Bid Manager's Handbook* provides an invaluable resource in the battle to win new business.

Taking an extremely practical approach and using real-life examples, David Nickson leads the reader through every stage of planning for, producing and delivering a bid. By the end of the book you will:

- know what needs to be done
- know how to present the information to the prospective client effectively
- have gained the writing and editorial skills needed to put a sales case across
- have identified the skills that are needed to manage a bid

Crucially it also shows how to save time – the most important commodity in any bid as it is always a scarce resource – without affecting quality. In short, *The Bid Manager's Handbook* is the definitive guide to managing winning bids effectively and efficiently.

GOWER

Project Management for Successful Product Innovation

Alan Webb

This comprehensive book provides a complete guide to managing projects involving the development of new products. It aims to give the practising project manager an insight into the many processes that are involved in handling one of the most complex of industrial activities.

The book is arranged in a logical sequence covering the development of project management, project management structures, aspects of planning, monitoring and control, economics and value management, design management, intellectual property issues and production start-up. Particular emphasis has been given to risk management which is recognized as both a difficult subject and also one of growing importance to today's project manager, especially in product innovation. A complete explanation is given of the latest and most relevant techniques together with guidance as to where and how they should be applied. Where software tools are available these are named and, in some cases, brief descriptions are included; in all cases contact details of the vendors are provided.

GOWER

Gower Handbook
of Project Management
Third Edition

J. Rodney Turner and Stephen J. Simister

This is a thoroughly revised and restructured edition of the highly successful *Gower Handbook of Project Management*. The new content is shaped by, and linked to, the body of knowledge produced by the International Project Management Association and the Project Management Institute of the USA, and so will be an invaluable study aid for anyone following either certification programme. In following this framework the book provides comprehensive coverage of the knowledge required both by practising project managers and by those wishing to study the subject.

The book is divided into seven parts covering:

- The systems of project management
- The context of projects including political, economic, social, technical, legal and environmental issues
- The management of performance including functionality, quality, time, cost, risk and safety
- The management of the project life-cycle
- The management of commercial issues including appraisal and finance
- The management of contracts
- The management of the people involved.

This unique encyclopaedia for the discipline and profession of project management is destined to become a classic that no-one in the field should be without.

GOWER

Gower Handbook
of Purchasing Management

Third Edition

Marc Day

Published in association with the *Chartered Institute of Purchasing and Supply*

The revised third edition of the *Gower Handbook of Purchasing Management* views procurement as standing on the boundary of the firm, looking outwards and scanning the environment for new opportunities and threats. In this respect, as in many others, the new edition is quite different from the previous two, reflecting the many changes that have taken place for businesses over the years. In particular this edition has been slimmed down and focused to assist the reader by working systematically outwards using a purchasing lens to view the wider business world. The aim is to show the potential contribution that purchasing can make as a driver for organizational efficiency and business development. It is this latter requirement, the need for purchasing to generate revenue, that has been identified as being ever more prominent as a demand on purchasing directors' time and effort.

The book is now split into three sections. Part I lays the foundations for building the organization of purchasing in a corporate environment. Part II overlays further applications on the foundations of purchasing organization. The assumption is made that the purchasing activities of a firm are proactive in outlook, gathering knowledge and measuring their current corporate purchasing performance, while also looking to generate revenues for the business. Finally Part III provides case studies which bring to life some of the learning achieved through the framework laid out in the previous parts.

Written by leading practitioners and academics, and published in association with the Chartered Institute of Purchasing and Supply, this book is destined to become a classic in the field.

GOWER